The Authorities

Powerful Wisdom from Leaders in the Field

PATRICK RAMSAY

Award-Winning Author

Copyright © 2021 Authorities Press

ISBN: 978-1-77277-415-3

All rights reserved. No portion of this book may be reproduced mechanically, electronically, or by any other means, including photocopying, without permission of the publisher or author except in the case of brief quotations embodied in critical articles and reviews. It is illegal to copy this book, post it to a website, or distribute it by any other means without permission from the publisher or author.

Limits of Liability and Disclaimer of Warranty

The author and publisher shall not be liable for your misuse of the enclosed material. This book is strictly for informational and educational purposes.

Warning – Disclaimer

The purpose of this book is to educate and entertain. The author and/or publisher do not guarantee that anyone following these techniques, suggestions, tips, ideas, or strategies will become successful. The author and/or publisher shall have neither liability nor responsibility to anyone with respect to any loss or damage caused, or alleged to be caused, directly or indirectly by the information contained in this book.

Medical Disclaimer

The medical or health information in this book is provided as an information resource only, and is not to be used or relied on for any diagnostic or treatment purposes. This information is not intended to be patient education, does not create any patient-physician relationship, and should not be used as a substitute for professional diagnosis and treatment.

Publisher
Authorities Press
Markham, ON
Canada

Printed in the United States, Canada, and the United Kingdom.

FOREWORD

Experts are to be admired for their knowledge, but they often remain unrecognized by the general public because they save their information and insights for paying customers and clients. There are many experts in a given field, but their impact is limited to the handful of people with whom they work.

Unlike experts, authorities share their knowledge and expertise far more broadly, so they make a big impact on the world. Authorities become known and admired as leading experts and, as such, typically do very well economically and professionally. Most authorities are also mature enough to know that part of the joy of monetary success is the accompanying moral and spiritual obligation to give back.

Many people want to learn and work with well-respected and generous authorities, but don't always know where to find them. They may be known to their peers, or within a specific community, but have not had the opportunity to reach a wider audience. At one time, they might have submitted a proposal to the *For Dummies* or *Chicken Soup for the Soul* series of books, but it's now almost impossible to get accepted as a new author in such a branded book series.

It is more than fitting that Raymond Aaron, an internationally known and respected authority in his own right, would be the one to recognize the need for a new venue in which authorities could share their considerable knowledge with readers everywhere. As the only author ever to be included in both of the book series mentioned above, Raymond has had the opportunity to give back and he understands how crucial it is for authorities to have a platform from which to share their expertise.

I have known and worked with Raymond for a number of years and consider him a valued friend and talented coach. He knows how to spot talented and knowledgeable people and he desires to see them prosper. Over the years, success coaching and speaking engagements around the world have made it possible for Raymond to meet many of these talented authorities. He recognizes and relates to their passion and enthusiasm for what they do, as well as their desire to share what they know. He tells me that's why he created this new nonfiction branded book series, *The Authorities*.

Dr. Nido Qubein
President, High Point University

TABLE OF CONTENTS

Introduction V

The Secret Language of Success 1
Patrick Ramsay

What You Don't Know About Money 19
Bob Proctor

Step Into Greatness 25
Les Brown

Unleashing Your Full Potential 35
Brian Tracy

Branding Small Business 45
Raymond Aaron

What the World Needs Now 57
Angela Golden Bryan

The Mindset of Success 71
Anna Griffin

Break Down the Box 95
Kirk Jakesta

Five Key Elements for Success 123
Alana Leone

Developing Resiliency in the Face of Adversity 145
Tim Deloso

You Are Not Your Scars™ 159
Ellie D. Shefi

Unlocking the Secret to Success 183
Rav Bains

INTRODUCTION

Welcome to *The Authorities*. This is an anthology of stories and ideas from individuals who have distinguished themselves in life and in business. They are people who leave big footprints on the world, and as leaders in their particular fields they also understand the importance and obligation of giving something back.

Authorities are not just experts. They are also known to be outstanding in their fields and in their communities. Because of this important difference, authorities are able to contribute more to humanity through both their chosen work and by giving back.

You will definitely know some of *The Authorities* in this book, especially since there are some world-famous ones. Others are just as exceptional, but you may not yet know about them.

Patrick Ramsay is the award-winning co-author of the book *The Authorities*. He is published alongside New York Times bestselling authors Bob Proctor, Les Brown, Brian Tracy and Raymond Aaron. Patrick has learned from these legends in wealth creation and motivational speaking. His mission is to share what the elite and extremely successful individuals know, and show you how to implement their secrets.

Growing up in a small, industrial town in western Canada, Patrick became a successful entrepreneur. He started many small businesses and then lost most of his money when he fell into the trap many of us fall into. He lost his way by believing he was someone other than who he really was. He spent the next eight years of his life in search of the real secret to success. On the journey to unveiling the steps, there were many surprises as to what was really going on behind the scenes. The answers were very shocking, but simple.

Patrick Ramsay is a successful entrepreneur in the investment world. He has a profitable real estate and investment portfolio that allows his money to work for him. As a coach, he shares his deep insight and wisdom with people all around the world. He helps them become money magnets and winners in the financial game of life, showing them how to avoid the pitfalls that can riddle their path. He has a unique ability to take knowledge and translate it into wisdom, so that anyone can understand the secrets of success and how they relate to each individual.

Patrick received an award for *The Authorities* series book from his publisher at his book launch in 2021. Later that same year, Patrick was recognized for the personal implementation of his teachings in his second book, *Postulate Like A Pro*, co-authored alongside the New York Times bestselling author Raymond Aaron.

Please read each chapter carefully to learn and to see the business possibilities that may exist between yourself and any of *The Authorities*. You could become their client or, perhaps, do business with them in other ways. Learn from them. Connect with them. Let them uplift you. Learning from them and working with them is a secret ingredient for success which may well allow you to rise to the level of Authority soon.

To be considered for inclusion in a subsequent edition of *The Authorities*, register to attend an event at www.aaron.com/events where you will be interviewed and considered.

The Secret Language of Success

PATRICK RAMSAY

In only 1 year, I was able to successfully change my finances and goals and turn my life around.

So now I have decided to dedicate my life to help you and others transition to a better life. I am ready to be your transition coach and I promise to bring inspiration to your transformation.

Interested? Read on…

While working a regular 9 to 5 job, I started a transportation company. I grew that company from $100,000 to $1 million in sales in less than a year. It took only 4 years for me to take that to $5 million. By then, I was 35, and it took me only 3 years to acquire millions in real estate. Now, I am extremely successful at trading stocks, forex, crypto and commodities. I am also an award-winning author. In my life, I have successfully transitioned 6 times from one career to another.

But it wasn't always like this.

After college, where I learned marketing management, I worked at a 9 to 5 job for four years. As I mentioned, I started a transportation business while at that job. For six months I continued to work there while I figured out all the logistics and financing for this business venture. When I was ready, I quite my 9 to 5 job and took my chances with the transportation business.

But this wasn't my first try at my own business. Like many people, I tried my hand at various ventures, hoping one of them would allow me to quit my job and make a good living. I had a firewood business, vending machines, and a skidder (a piece of equipment that pulls logs through the bush). They all did okay. I made money. Looking back, though, I realize that I didn't put 110% effort in any of them. I was just playing around. Testing the waters to see if something would happen.

THE RIGHT MINDSET

I plan to not only help people hit their financial goals in business, but also to have the right mindset when they get there so that they don't lose it all soon after. Just teaching the financial end of business is like the school system teaching children about mathematics and grammar, but not practical things like how to manage your finances or change a flat tire. It needs to be a balanced approach.

It's like taking care of a physical ailment by popping pills that alleviate the pain without figuring out the cause. You will eventually have major problems to deal with.

I'm not just selling a course to teach you how to make it in real estate or the stock market. I was able to start 9 different businesses and become successful in each. This is to show you that I have figured out how to use what I've learned to become successful in potentially any type of business.

Anyone can be successful at any business they love to do if they know why they are doing it. I just worked for money in the beginning. I felt like I had no choice with the amount of debt I had. Most people are in the same boat. Once I reached $1 million in my transportation business, I thought, "Is this it?" Then I created my next target of $3 million. When I reached that, I had the same question. I created my next target of $5 million. When I reached that, I once again asked the question, "Is this it?" Not only did this happen 3 times, it got worse each time. An emptiness of wondering if there wasn't something better that I was supposed to feel.

Not long after reaching the $5 million mark, my business crashed. It wasn't sudden but I didn't see it coming. In no time, I was $1 million in debt and had to sell all the equipment I had, to drop the debt down to $700,000.

My father died when I was 31. I was without a job, $700,000 in debt, with no idea how to pay it off. I had to sell my vehicle and my house and move into the basement of my in-laws with my wife and two young children. I had no way to pay for any courses to learn new skills and had no idea what I wanted to do. I was very depressed and worried I might have to claim bankruptcy.

If you only work for the money, you never get the why. I realized that I wasn't looking at the why. I didn't know what my why was for making those targets, let alone how to hit them.

In reality, it's not reaching the goal which is the most fulfilling. It is the journey. This applies to everything in life including finance. It's not reaching the target of $1 million but the process of getting there. But you never know that while you're going through it. That's why a coach can be invaluable. They're great for reminding you to enjoy the journey.

WHERE I AM NOW

I currently have a large real estate portfolio that is managed mostly by property managers. I spend my days investing in stocks and cryptocurrencies. I have a choice now of how I spend my days. I don't have to do the standard 9 to 5 anymore.

I choose what I spend my time on and whom I spend it with. I choose coaching. I love it. I love helping others get to a point in their lives where they can also make that choice of what to do in their day. Doing what makes them happy, what feeds their passion.

I want to give back and help you become successful without having to go through the pain that I went through.

Many people go to business coaches to learn how to make their millions, or for some other materialistic reason. But that's a superficial approach. Helping you find your drive to find the why is the first step to take, instead of just looking at the number at the end.

BECOMING A BILLIONAIRE IN AN HOUR

Just focusing on how to get rich without finding your why has pitfalls. Its why I felt empty and why others have become depressed. One of the first exercises I do with my clients is something called 'becoming a billionaire in one hour.' It's a fast journey to show you the billionaire mindset. Once you see that money is not an object, you start to look at what you have left. Going through this exercise, you look at why you want to be there. That was my hardest lesson to learn.

You can come to me to learn how to become a successful real estate, stock market, crypto investor, or increase your current business or career income. I'll help you to do that. Along the way, you'll discover yourself and you'll be able to say, "Now I know why." Once you know your why, everything else falls into place. You don't necessarily think about the money aspect. It just seems to appear.

On the road to becoming a billionaire, we start with $1. How would you spend that $1? That dollar increases exponentially. How would you spend $2, $4, etc.? Once you've reached $1 million, $10 million, $20 million, you're really struggling to spend every dime. It's at that point, when you start spending that huge amount of money, that it starts to feel empty. Unless you have that physical journey and experience in getting that money, you start to wonder what the money is for. I like to get this out of people's systems right away. We're going to make you a billionaire. How are you going to be different?

YOUR BELIEFS

I can teach you to achieve your financial targets such as making $1 million. But if your belief is that you can only make $60,000, you'll find a way to lose that million and go back to the $60,000 level. You'll be able to overcome that initial belief you have for a time, especially with the help of a coach or other training. However, once you've taken your foot off the pedal, your beliefs will take over again and bring you down to the level at which you feel comfortable.

It works both ways. If you go down to $40,000 a year, your beliefs kick in and you get your ass in gear to get back to the $60,000 a year level you believe, subconsciously, that is where you belong.

That's what bothered me when I went through my cycle of success and failure. How could I go from nothing to a few million and then back down to zero, even $700,000 in the hole? It turns out that it's not an uncommon thing with millionaires.

HITTING BOTTOM

I discovered that once you hit the bottom, there are certain things that happen to you and there are things you need to change.

Often, it's only at the bottom that you realize you've had a belief about yourself and how things should be. It's usually not until this point that most of you can either question or discard your beliefs.

It's raw at the bottom. It's black and white.

But with the help of a coach, you can get rid of the beliefs that are limiting you–before you go all the way down. Isn't that worth the price of admission?

Think of someone who smoked most of their life and is told by their doctor to either quit or die. That's bottom. That's where you can question and discard beliefs because your necessity level is very high and can help you alter your beliefs.

Being able to show you those changes without dropping that far is a big part of what I do. I still encourage you to make mistakes. Unfortunately, we don't learn as much from our successes, compared to our failures. I give my kids this same information. They are encouraged to learn and make their own mistakes. Creativity is experimentation. You don't always get it right when you experiment.

My daughter has a keen interest in fitness and health. She's created a fitness and meal plan for my wife who's shown it to her friends. The interest in my daughter's new 'business' is growing rapidly. It's a great endeavour she'll learn from as she makes mistakes, and has successes. And I'll be there the whole time, coaching, guiding, and supporting her.

YOU SHOULD NEVER STOP LEARNING

The belief that coaching or mentoring is not as important later in life as it is when we're going through grade school is ridiculous. Most people get to grade 12 or finish college, get a job and stop learning. But that's exactly when the real learning should start.

We all know that traditional school doesn't equip you with the knowledge and experience you need as an entrepreneur or certain life skills. If you're able to learn from someone who has done it, as opposed to having to struggle through it as I did, it's a major benefit. To do well in business, you're told to be different and stand out, whereas in school you're forced to follow the rules and be like everyone else. The two don't work well together.

There's more than enough knowledge out there in this day and age. You need coaching to use that knowledge to encourage action and realize wisdom. It forces you to focus. Coaching increases your desire and necessity level without having to drop so low. My coaching is there to ignite a passion that will motivate you to take action towards your transformation.

The term coach might be a bit overused. It's almost better to say guide because I'm walking with you as you try to find your way (and sometimes stumble). I show you a route through the hazards. Once you can see that, you can finally take the blindfold off and say, "I didn't realize it was this simple."

Once you're shown, it's quite different. It's life-changing. It's transformational. I coach the mechanics of business but also of the mindset. I know the pitfalls and can steer you away from them while I show them to you. That is very difficult to find in books. You almost have to see it as it happens.

YOU ARE A MONEY MAGNET

Even if you already make a million dollars, there's another level. It's not about the money anymore. That's what you need to realize. Money is something that comes because of what's inside of you. It's not because of what's out there. You are a money magnet. When that magnet is weak, it's because of your beliefs. Your inner self is causing your magnet to be weak.

The stronger your insides, the stronger your magnet outside, and the more you attract things that are positive. But that also works in the other direction. I went from being a millionaire to being a million dollars in debt. It was at this point that I got my insight. That's what started me on this journey. I've been able to repeat it now a few times. To improve, I got coaching. It helped me tremendously.

Why do we resist going to school or getting coached? Because of the cost? I can tell you that I've made 20, 30, 40 times more than what my coaching cost. Getting people to understand that is part of the process. If you can't believe enough to take that step, you may not be ready to grow. If you pay and believe, you're already getting coached. If you don't take that step and make excuses, you get what you deserve. Because you're never wrong. Every decision you make is right. And your belief determines what you get.

TAKING THE NEXT STEP

It's one of the following three things that keep you from taking that next step: fear, self-doubt, or your beliefs. Have you ever seen the video of Will Smith preparing for his first parachute jump out of an airplane? He walks us through all his trials and tribulations while he gets ready for the jump. He says that the only time to be afraid is when you step off the plane. Yet most of us build up an unbelievable fear, well before the point of jumping off.

It doesn't matter how smart you are or how much knowledge you have. It's whether you take action. You don't want to let fear keep you from making a move. That's the other part of the equation. Coaching is the action aspect. Things will present themselves in life that you need to act on. Fear wants to hold you back. That fear is powerful and won't allow you to take the next step. That's why people don't get ahead.

They don't seize the opportunity because they don't have all the answers. That's what they tell themselves. But that's not how life is supposed to work. You're not supposed to know everything. You're not supposed to know every single step. The journey is the important part. It's not the end goal. It's who you become. It's not what you get when you're done.

Once you learn these drills, these steps, you'll be able to teach them to anybody. I've taught my teenage son. He's created a trading course, and has many people signed up to train on how to trade. It's action. He's taken the step even with the fear. He isn't waiting until he knows everything. He's not an accountant or financial whiz. He doesn't have all the knowledge. He's just a kid, but he's taking action. He has me guiding him just like any father would. The difference is that I'm also a coach. I can answer his questions from experience not just as a father. I help him take action through his fear because he has confidence that I can guide him.

Action and follow-through are most important. Don't wait until you have all the answers and knowledge. Get a coach to help you take your first step or your next step. Don't let your fear come up with excuses that keep you from starting or moving forward. Get a coach to guide you and give you the confidence to get moving.

THE ROLLER COASTER

If making that first million dollars made me feel empty inside, obviously, it's not what I really wanted. I thought the million dollars would make me a happier person. I thought it was my goal. I thought it was everyone's goal. Isn't that what everyone wants? Or is it like the dog that chases a car? What happens when it catches the car? The fun chase is over. The dog is no longer happy, excited, and full of life. It's kind of confused and doesn't know what to do.

People may want a million dollars but, when they get it, they often find that it wasn't really the million dollars that they wanted after all. But that's not something you can explain to people. They can't know it until they have the million dollars. They have to be in the right frame of mind. They come in thinking that I'm going to help them get their first million dollars. I'm not necessarily moving away from that. I'm refining it. It eventually comes out that it's not the million dollars.

It's your internal healing that determines your external environment. If you feel bad, you have a bad environment. If you feel good, you have a good environment.

MONEY AMPLIFIES YOUR SUBCONSCIOUS

What I see happening to people that hit their financial targets is a multiplying of their personalities. In other words, hitting a million dollars is going to make you 10 times the person you are now–good or bad. If you're generous and loving, you'll be ten times more generous and loving. If you're an angry person, it's just going to make you angrier. The money will amplify the type of person you are right now. If there's an emptiness inside you, money won't fill that void; it will multiply that empty feeling. This is where I ended up initially.

It's very important to start from the right position because making money is going to amplify who you really are. This is a big part of what I learned, the hard way. The more I made, the emptier I got. The more miserable I got. The more I created a negative environment, which finally led me to be $1 million in the hole. I didn't see or understand that emptiness before I started. But it became very obvious the more my revenue increased.

THE JOURNEY

You might not think that working on your beliefs and your why should be in a book about business coaching. That is why I like to call it The Secret Language of Success. It encompasses more than just making money. It includes keeping the money and, as a bonus, being a happier person. Realize that any journey towards a desired goal will contain pain, struggle, and sacrifice. The bigger the goal, or more accurately, the further the goal is from your present situation, the more the difficulties and barriers. The journey is the rewarding part. The goal simply allows you to know when you are finished this particular journey.

If your internal environment is low, you don't see opportunities as you would if you were feeling good.

You could be walking down the street thinking about how you're ready to work with a coach, get some help and move up to a new level of success. Then you bump into me. I tell you my story and you think how fantastic that is. What a coincidence. And we end up working together. That would be because of your good internal environment.

On the other hand, you could be walking down the street with a mantra of "I want a million dollars" going through your mind. We bump into each other. I tell you my story. And you simply move on, continuing your mantra – you have a low internal environment.

That's the difference in life right there. When your belief appears, action needs to be taken. Most people don't do that. They don't have all the answers yet and so don't take action. It doesn't matter which path you take. Which path you choose is not important. It's important to take a path and get moving.

Fortunately, the people I work with they don't necessarily see that I'm working on them at the same time as we're working on getting them to their financial targets. I'm not just getting them to $1 million (if that's their goal).

I'm helping them get and keep their target by making it their new belief.

I help people achieve their targets while at the same time changing their beliefs so they don't go back to their old beliefs as soon as they take their foot off the pedal.

HOW I COACH

I don't have to do this coaching. I am not doing it for the money. It's simply important for me to give back and help others achieve their goals without going through the unnecessary, painful crashes that often happen.

When someone is at a low emotional level, you can't teach them anything. All you can do is bring them up to a level where you can teach them. If a person wants to learn, he or she is already at a higher level.

I couldn't walk back into that 9 to 5 job I worked at years ago. The employees there hate their jobs but see it as a necessary evil. I wouldn't be able to tell them the information that's in this chapter. It wouldn't resonate with them. They would tune out.

If I told them that I worked at this very same company and got myself out by starting my own business and everything is great, they might not realize that what I would be able to help them. If I told them that I did well, then the business crashed, but I figured things out and am ready to teach others what I learned, they might want to learn more.

With teaching comes improvement in the person and a connection with the coach. This is where the highest level of teaching can be transferred. This is the most enjoyable and rewarding part for me, and it's the biggest gain for you.

People can still come to me with the goal of making a million dollars, but they'll come away with much more. They'll still have the potential to make the million, but they'll get there from a very positive psychological or spiritual place.

I'm not here to give you knowledge. I'm here to teach wisdom. I'm not trying to give you information that you can get from the internet. I'm helping you with something that is very difficult to get on your own. If you try to do it on your own, it comes at a high price. Much higher than mine. Plus, I'm there with you to work through the emotional lows before they can take over your actions.

My secret isn't the knowledge. It's the process. I'm not a motivational speaker who spends a lot of time pumping you up with your potential. That only lasts as long as I'm motivating you. That's not my style of coaching. I'm not trying to make you feel good as quickly as possible. That's more of an artificial happiness, as opposed to a more genuine, ingrained feeling. I'm here to help you feel good properly, through the gaining of wisdom and working through your current beliefs towards the beliefs you truly want. I take you along a life path instead of just a holiday. Unfortunately, that takes you out of your comfort zone for a time.

Doing the hard steps and getting out of your comfort zone is difficult on your own. Reading self-help books, watching motivational speakers, or listening to their CDs is helpful but a coach can keep you on track and assist with decision-making. You don't want to wait until you hit rock bottom to get out of your comfort zone. You can then do it on your own if your necessity level is high enough, but it's an extremely arduous route. I know. I took it.

I'll make sure you're taking action and moving forward. If you're able to open your mind even a little bit to what I'm doing, I'll open it more and fill it with the beliefs you want so they actually come true. Not fill it with more knowledge to make you feel good. Knowledge is useless unless you make it yours and use it. I make sure you use your knowledge.

There are certain steps I take with each client, but because everyone is different, not everyone's step is the first step. That's where coaching becomes 1 on 1. Everyone is different and handled differently, but everyone ends up going through the same steps eventually.

COMMUNICATION LANGUAGE

There are four different types of languages people understand. This is based on the Kolbe Index www.kolbe.com. If I don't give you what you want to hear in your language, you won't understand me, and it won't be the experience you want. This is key to being able to be understood as a teacher or coach. I need to communicate with you in your language or you won't respond well. That's where some of the failures come in with students. I can't properly teach you something if I say it in my language, not yours.

It is how people listen, speak, and react. How they interpret information or instructions. This is a behavior driven by your instinct. The four language modes are:

Fact Finder: How much information do you need to understand? Do you want the overview or need as many specifics as possible?

Follow-through: How do you organize information? Do you develop shortcuts or create a system?

Quick Start: How fast are you to act on something? Do you stick with what works or make stuff up and try new things?

Implementer: How do you get started? Do you picture things in your mind or do you construct tangible solutions?

For example - I do not need many facts; I don't like systems; I try new things and I fix things when they break.

Whereas school molds you, coaching should mold to you. You have to understand the language of the other person and talk to them in their language (not yours) or they will not understand what you are saying, and may just stop listening. I get an understanding of where you fit in each of the four categories, and communicate at those levels as best I can. If someone wants facts, I need to give them facts because if I give them a brief overview, they will think that I am flaky and hiding something. On the other hand, if they want an overview and I give them facts they stop listening, and want to leave and have nothing to do with me.

A coach-client relationship is an opportunity for the coach to learn the client's language so the coach can maximize the amount of information the coach is able to get across to the client.

ARE YOU READY TO REACH OUT?

Until your mind is open and ready to hear this information, you won't be able to get away from this roller-coaster ride that swings between going above and below your beliefs like a yoyo. Sadly, it seems like the only place to be able to do this on your own is when you are at your lowest and you figure that you have nothing to lose. No one wants to wait until they hit that point before they make the necessary changes to live a better life.

You don't want your mind to be cracked open from hitting the bottom.

You want to be opening your own mind before hitting that low point. That's where I want to help educate and guide you to discover your beliefs. I want to help you get to a place where you can receive the information you need because you're ready to receive it.

As a coach, I have to resonate with that interest while you open your mind. Now I can communicate. You can receive, and believe you can achieve your goals.

If you are willing to work with me to bring yourself to a point where your internal environment is good, and ready for your next level of training, I will gladly guide you towards the goals that are part of your hopes and dreams.

To learn more about real estate, stock market, crypto investing, and increasing your business and career income, please visit Patrick Ramsay's website at transitionmaster.com and go to the contact page and request a 30min free session with Patrick.

What You Don't Know About Money

BOB PROCTOR

There was a time when I didn't feel very comfortable talking about money. So, I never had very much of it. I've since learned that money can't talk but it can hear, and if you call it, it will come. When I started to get comfortable with the idea of money, everything changed. And before long, I knew I'd never have to worry about money again Would you like to eliminate that worry from your life, once and for all?

There's no question that you can do it if you understand the truth about:

- What money is
- How to earn a substantial income
- How to guarantee a steady and sizeable stream of income

Let's talk about each one of those things to help you get on the path to living a life of your choosing, rather than accepting the life you have.

WHAT MONEY IS

Money is not the paper you carry around in your wallet or purse. Those dollar bills—no matter what denomination they are—merely represent money.

Money is an idea; it's a reward received for a service rendered. The more service you provide, the more money you have, and the more you can do in the world.

Money is an instrument that serves two purposes. First, it makes you comfortable. The more money you have, the more comfortable you are, and the more creative you become. And second, it enables you to extend the service you provide far beyond your own presence.

By way of example, let's say that you want to feed the hungry. You can feed far more people with $50,000 than you can with $100. Having more money makes you more effective at whatever you want to do.

HOW TO EARN A SUBSTANTIAL INCOME

Like it or not, money will have a greater influence on your life than almost any other commodity you can think of. The good news is all the money in the universe is available to you. But you've got to earn it. And you earn it by providing a service. Everything in the world operates by natural laws, including how much money you earn. In fact, there's a law that governs how much money you and I will earn. It's called the Law of Compensation.

This Law clearly states the amount of money you earn will always be in exact ratio to:

1. **The need for what you do.** People who are paying you for products or services put a specific value on your contribution. The greater the need is for what you do, the higher your value will be. Of course, not everyone who works in a field where there's a high need earns a high income. That's where the second factor of the Law of Compensation comes in.

2. **Your ability to do it.** When you work in a field where there is a tremendous need, and you become very good at filling that need, your compensation goes way up. To command a high salary in any job or position, you have to master what you do. And that brings us to the third and final factor of the Law.

3. **The difficulty there will be in replacing you.** If there are five equally qualified and motivated people who want your job, and they can do your job equally well, you have very low leverage in negotiating a good or better salary. If, on the other hand, it would take your employer months to get someone even half as qualified to do your job as well as you, your employer will pay you top dollar because you're going to be very difficult to replace.

No matter how much money you want to earn, these three factors determine the amount of money or its equivalent you will get for your work.

However, if you concentrate your efforts on the second factor—your ability to do the work—and you become a master at what you do, you will receive the highest rewards.

HOW TO GUARANTEE A STEADY AND SIZEABLE STREAM OF INCOME

When the average person looks at the very wealthy—billionaires or even millionaires—he or she assumes there's something special about them, that they're more intelligent and savvier than 'normal people.' This assumption is both true and false.

Wealthy people are 'normal people' who have a different mindset than the masses; they have thoroughly internalized the mindset of wealth. They're rich because they've made a decision to be, and they've developed a prosperity consciousness. Their mind is clear, and they expect wealth. Nothing causes them to pause or hesitate. They don't worry about failure because, in their mind's eye, all they see is being successful.

And here's one more thing that sets wealthy people apart from the masses: They employ the easiest and most sound way to enjoy financial freedom—Multiple Sources of Income (MSI).

MSI are passive revenue streams coming in that are beyond the income from your current job, vocation, career, or livelihood. Creating passive revenue streams allows you to make money around the clock, whether you're working or not.

Of course, MSI don't create wealth overnight. It takes some time to achieve financial freedom. However, it takes only one well-executed big idea to harvest six or seven figures from MSI.

That doesn't mean you have to hit the ball out of the park on the first swing. If your first attempt only generates a few hundred dollars a month, that's a significant step in the right direction. It doesn't mean that it's all you can do or the best you can do—it's just the first step, and you can build from there.

ACT NOW!

All the money in the universe is available to you, but you have to earn it.

Earl Nightingale said, "Most people think they want more money than they really do, and they settle for a whole lot less than they could get."

Do you know how much money you need to live the way you truly want to live? Sit down with a pen, let your imagination flow, and figure it out. When you've come up with a figure that will make you happy, write it down.

Now that you know what money is, how to earn a lot of it, how to guarantee a steady and sizeable income steam whether you're working or not, and how much money you need to earn, what's next?

Many people say knowledge is power, but they're wrong. Knowledge is only potential power.

To become wealthy, you have to do more than know how to do it. You must apply that knowledge by taking steps now that will allow you to start earning more, and continuously move closer to your goal.

Step Into Greatness

LES BROWN

You have greatness within you. You can do more than you could ever imagine. The problem most people have is that they set a goal and then ask, "how can I do it? I don't have the necessary skills or education or experience."

I know what that's like. I wasted 14 years on asking myself how I could be a motivational speaker. My mind focused on the negative—on the things that were in my way, rather than on the things that were not.

It's not what you don't have but what you think you need that keeps you from getting what you want from life. But, when the dream is big enough, the obstacles don't matter. You'll get there if you stay the course. Nothing can stop you but death itself.

Think about that last statement for a minute. There's nothing on this earth that can stop you from achieving what it is that you want. So, get out of your way, and quit sabotaging your dreams. Do everything in your power to make them happen—because you cannot fail!

They say the best way to die is with your loved ones gathered around your bed. But what if you were dying and it was the ideas you never acted upon, the gifts you never used and the dreams you never pursued, that were circled around your bed? Answer that question right now. Write down your answers. If you die this very moment, what ideas, what gifts, what dreams will die with you?

Then say: I refuse to die an unlived life! You beat out 40 million sperm to get here, and you'll never have to face such odds again. Walk through the field of life and leave a trail behind.

One day, one of my rich friends brought my mother a new pair of shoes for me. Now, even though we weren't well off, I didn't want them; they were a size nine and I was a size nine and a half. My mother didn't listen and told my sister to go get some Vaseline, which she rubbed all over my feet. Then my mother had me put those shoes on, minding that I didn't scrunch down the heel. She had my sister run some water in the bathtub, and I was told to get in and walk around in the water. I said that my feet hurt. She just ignored me and asked about my day at school, how everything went and did I get into any fights? I knew what she was up to, that she was trying to distract me, so I said I had only gotten into three fights. After a while mother asked me if my feet still hurt. I admitted that the pain had indeed lessened. She kept me walking in that tub until I had a brand new pair of comfortable, size nine and a half shoes.

You see, once the leather in the shoes got wet, they stretched! And what you need to do is stretch a little. I believe that most people don't set high goals and miss them, but rather, they set lower goals and hit them and then they stay there, stuck on the side of the highway of life. When you're pursuing your greatness, you don't know what your limitations are, and you need to act like you don't have any. If you shoot for the moon and miss, you'll still be in the stars.

You also need coaching (a mentor). Why? There are times you, too, will find yourself parked on the side of the highway of life with no gas in the vehicle. What you need then is someone to stop and offer to pick up some gas down the road a ways and bring it back to you. That person is your coach. Yes, they are there for advice, but their main job is to help you through the difficulties that life throws at all of us.

Another reason for having a coach is that you can't see the picture when you're in the frame. In other words, he or she can often see where you are with a clarity and focus that's unavailable to you. They're not going to leave you parked along the road of life, nor are they going to allow you to be stuck in the moment like a photo in a frame.

And let's say you just can't see your way forward. You don't believe it's possible. Sometimes you just have to believe in someone's belief in you. This could be your coach, a loved one, or even a staunch friend. You need to hear them say you can do it, time and again. Because, after all, faith comes from hearing and hearing and hearing.

Look at it this way. Most people fail because of possibility blindness. They can't see what lies before them. There are always possibilities. Because of this, your dream is possible. You may fail often. In fact, I want you to say this: I will fail my way to success. Here is why.

I had a TV show that failed. I felt I had to go back to public speaking. I had failed, so I parked my car for 10 years. Then I saw Dr. Wayne Dyer was still on PBS and I decided to call them. They said they would love to work with me and asked where I had been. I wasn't as good as I had been 10 years before, as I was out of practice, but I still had to get back in the game. I was determined to drive on empty.

Listen to recordings, go to seminars, challenge yourself, and you'll begin to step into your greatness; you'll begin to fill yourself with the energy you need to climb to greater heights. Most people never attend a seminar. They won't invest money in books or audio programs. You put yourself in the top five percent just by making a different choice than the average person. This is called contrary thinking. It's a concept taken from the financial industry. One considers choosing the exact opposite behaviour of the average person as a way to get better than average results. You don't have to make the contrarian choice, but if you don't have anything to lose by going that road, why not consider the option?

Make your move before you're ready. Walk by faith, not by sight, and make sure you're happy doing it. If you can't be happy, what else is there? Helen Keller said, "Life is short, eat the dessert first."

What is faith? Many of us think of God when we think of faith. A different viewpoint claims that faith is a firm belief in something for which there is no proof. I would rather think of faith as something that is believed especially with strong conviction. It is this last definition I am referring to when I say walk by faith, not by sight. Be happy and go forth with strong conviction that you are destined for greatness.

An important step on your way to greatness is to take the time to detoxify. You've got to look at the people in your life. What are they doing for you? Are they setting a pace that you can follow? If not, whose pace have you adjusted to? If you're the smartest in your group, find a new group.

Are the people in your life pulling you down or lifting you up? You know what to do, right? Banish the negative and stay with the positive; it's that simple. Dr. Norman Vincent Peale once said (when I was in the audience), "You are special. You have greatness within you, and you can do more than you could ever possibly imagine."

He overrode the inner conversations in my mind and reached the heart of me. He set me on fire. This is yet another reason for seeking out the help of a coach or mentor, or other new people in your life. They can do what Dr. Peale did for me. They can set your passion free.

How important is it to have the right kind of person/people on your side? There was a study done that determined it takes 16 people saying you can do something to overcome one person who says you can't do something. That's right, one negative, unsupportive person can wipe out the work of 16 other supportive people. The message can't be any clearer than that.

Let's face the cold, hard truth: most people stay in park along the highway of life. They never feel the passion, the love for their fellow man, or for the work they do. They are stuck in the proverbial rut. What's the reason? There are many reasons, but only one common factor: fear—fear of change, fear of failure, fear of success, fear they may not be good enough, fear of competition, even fear of rejection.

"Rejection is a myth," says Jack Canfield, co-author of The Chicken Soup for the Soul series. "It's not like you get a slap in the face each time you are rejected." Why not take every "no" you receive as a vitamin, and every time you take one, know you are another step closer to success.

You will win if you don't quit. Even a broken clock is right twice a day.

Professional baseball players, on average, get on base just three times out of every 10 times they face the opposing pitcher. Even superstars fail half of the time they appear at the plate.

Top commissioned salespeople face similar odds. They may make one sale from every three people they see, but it will have taken them between 75 and 100 telephone calls to make the 15 appointments they need to close their five sales for the week. And these are statistics for the elite. Most salespeople never reach these kinds of numbers.

People don't spend their lives working for just one company anymore. This means you must build up a set of skills and experiences that are portable. This can be done a number of ways, but my favorite approaches follow.

You must be willing to do the things others won't do, in order to have tomorrow the things that others don't have. Provide more service than you get paid for. Set some high standards for yourself.

Begin each day with your most difficult task. The rest of the day will seem more enjoyable and a whole lot easier.

Someone needs help with a problem? Be the solution to that problem.

Also, find those tasks that are being consistently ignored and do them. You'll be surprised by the results. An acquaintance of mine used this approach at a number of entry-level positions and each time he quickly ended up being offered a position in management.

You must increase your energy. Kick it up a notch. We are spirits having a physical existence; let your spirit shine. Quit frittering away your energy. Use it to move you closer to the achievement of your dreams. Refuse to spend it on non-productive activities.

What do people say about you when you leave a room? Are you willing to take responsibility—to walk your talk. There is a terrible epidemic sweeping our nation, and it is the refusal to take responsibility for one's actions. Consider that at some point in any situation there will have been a moment where you could have done something to change the outcome. To that end, you are responsible for what happened. It's a hard thing to accept, but it's true.

Life's hard. It was hard when I was told I had cancer. I had sunken into despair, and was hiding away in my study when my son came in. My son asked me if I was going to die. What could I do? I told him I was going to fight, even though I was scared. I also told him that I needed some help. Not because I was weak, but because I wanted to stay strong. Keep asking until you get help. Don't stop until you get it.

A setback is the setup for a comeback. A setback is simply a misstep on the long road of success. It means nothing in the larger scheme of things. And, surprisingly, it sets you up for your next win. It tends to focus you and your energy on your immediate goals, paving the way for your next sprint, for your comeback.

It's worth it. Your dreams are worth the sacrifices you'll have to make to achieve them. Find five reasons that will make your dreams worth it for you. Say to yourself, I refuse to live an unlived life.

If you are casual about your dreams, you'll end up a casualty. You must be passionate about your dreams, living and breathing them throughout your days. You've got to be hungry! People who are hungry refuse to take no for an answer. Make NO your vitamin. Be unstoppable. Be hungry. Let me give you an example of what I mean by hungry:

I decided I wanted to become a disc jockey, so I went down to the local radio station and asked the manager, Mr. Milton "Butterball" Smith, if he had a job available for a disc jockey. He said he did not. The next day I went back, and Mr. Smith asked, "Weren't you here yesterday?" I explained that I was just checking to see if anyone was sick or had died. He responded by telling me not to come back again. Day three, I went back again—with the same story. Mr. Smith told me to get out of there. I came back the fourth day and gave Mr. Smith my story one more time. He was so beside himself that he told me to get him a cup of coffee. I said, "Yes, sir!" That's how I became the errand boy.

While working as an errand boy at the station, I took every opportunity to hang out with the disc jockeys and to observe them working. After I had taught myself how to run the control room, it was just a matter of biding my time.

Then one day an opportunity presented itself. One of the disc jockeys by the name of Rockin' Roger was drinking heavily while he was on the air. It was a Saturday afternoon. And there I was, the only one there.

I watched him through the control-room window. I walked back and forth in front of that window like a cat watching a mouse, saying "Drink, Rock, Drink!" I was young. I was ready. And I was hungry.

Pretty soon, the phone rang. It was the station manager. He said, "Les, this is Mr. Klein."

I said, "Yes, I know."

He said, "Rock can't finish his program."

I said, "Yes sir, I know."

He said, "Would you call one of the other disc jockeys to fill in?"

Unleashing Your Full Potential

BRIAN TRACY

One of the qualities of "Authorities," of superior men and women, is that they are extremely self-reliant. They accept complete responsibility for themselves and everything that happens to them. They look to themselves as the source of their successes, and as the main cause of their problems and difficulties. High achievers say, "If it's to be, it's up to me." When things aren't moving along as fast as they want, they ask themselves, "What is it in me that is causing this problem?" They refuse to make excuses or to blame people. Instead, they look for ways to overcome obstacles and to make progress.

Totally self-responsible people look upon themselves as self-employed. They see themselves as the presidents of their own personal services corporations. They realize that no matter who signs their paycheck, in the final analysis, they work for themselves. Because they have this attitude of self-employment, they take a strategic approach to their work.

The essential element in strategic planning for a corporation or a business entity is the concept of "return on equity." All business planning is aimed at organizing and reorganizing the resources of the business in such a way as to increase the financial returns to the business owners. It is to increase the quantity of output relative to the quantity of input. It is to focus on areas of high profitability and return and simultaneously, to withdraw resources from areas of low profitability and low return. Companies that do this effectively in a rapidly changing environment are the ones that survive and prosper. Companies that fail to do this form of strategic analysis are those that fall behind and often disappear.

INCREASE YOUR RETURN ON ENERGY

To achieve everything you are capable of achieving as a person, you also must become a skilled strategic planner with regard to your life and work. But instead of aiming to increase your return on equity, your goal is to increase your return on energy.

Most people in our society start off in life with little more than their ability to work. More than 80 percent of the millionaires in North America started with little or nothing. Most people have been broke, or nearly broke, several times during their young-adult years. But the ones who eventually get ahead are those who do certain things in certain ways, over and over. These actions set them apart from the masses.

Perhaps the most important thing they do, consciously or unconsciously, is to look at themselves strategically, thinking about how they can better use themselves in the marketplace, how they can best capitalize on their strengths and abilities to increase their financial returns to themselves and their families.

INCREASE YOUR EARNING ABILITY

Your most valuable financial asset is your earning ability, your ability to earn money. Properly applied to the marketplace, it's like a pump. By exploiting your earning ability, you can pump tens of thousands of extra dollars a year into your pocket. All your knowledge, education, skills and experience contribute toward your earning ability, your ability to get results for which someone will pay you good money.

Your earning ability is like farmland. If you don't take excellent care of it, if you don't fertilize it and cultivate it and water it on a regular basis, it soon loses its ability to produce the kind of harvest that you desire. Successful men and women are those who are extremely aware of the importance and value of their earning ability, and they work every day to keep it growing and current with the demands of the marketplace.

One of your greatest responsibilities in life is to identify, develop and maintain an important marketable skill. It is to become very good at doing something for which there is a strong market demand.

DEVELOP A COMPETITIVE ADVANTAGE

In corporate strategy, we call this the development of a "competitive advantage." For a company, a competitive advantage is defined as an area of excellence in producing a product or service that gives the company a distinct edge over its competition.

In capitalizing on your strengths, as the president of your own personal services corporation, you also must have a clear competitive advantage. You also must have an area of excellence. You must do something that makes you different from and better than your competitors.

Your ability to identify and develop this competitive advantage is the most important thing you do in the world of work. It's the key to maintaining your earning ability. It's the foundation of your financial success. Without it, you're simply a pawn in a rapidly changing environment. But with a distinct competitive advantage, based on your strengths and abilities, you can write your own ticket. You can take charge of your own life. You can always get a job. And the more distinct your competitive advantage, the more money you can earn and the more places in which you can earn it.

FOUR KEYS TO COMPETITIVE ADVANTAGE

There are four keys to the strategic marketing of yourself and your services. These are applicable to huge companies such as General Motors, to candidates running for election, and to individuals who want to accomplish the very most in the very shortest period of time.

The first of these four keys is specialization. No one can be all things to all people. A "jack-of-all-trades" is also a "master of none." That career path usually leads to a dead end. Specialization is the key. Men and women who are successful have a series of general skills, but they also have one or two areas where they have developed the ability to perform in an outstanding manner.

Your decision about how, where, when and why you are going to specialize in a particular area of endeavor is perhaps the most important decision you will ever make in your career. It was well said that if you don't think about the future, you can't have one. The major reason why so many people are finding their jobs eliminated, and finding themselves unemployed for long periods of time, is because they didn't look down the road of life far enough and prepare themselves well enough for the time when their current jobs would expire. They suddenly found themselves out of gas on a lonely road, facing a long walk back to regular and well-paying employment. Don't let this happen to you.

In determining your area of specialization, put your current job aside for the moment, and take the time to look deeply into yourself. Analyze yourself from every point of view. Rise above yourself, and look at your lifetime of activities and accomplishments in determining what your area of specialization could be or should be.

You might be doing exactly the right job for you at this moment. You might already be capitalizing on all your strengths, and your current work might be ideally suited to your likes and dislikes, to your temperament and your personality. Nevertheless, you owe it to yourself to be continually expanding the scope of your vision and looking toward the future to see where you might want to be going in the months and years ahead. Remember, the best way to predict the future is to create it.

You possess special talents and abilities that make you unique, different from anyone else who has ever lived. The odds of there being another person just like you are more than 50 billion to one. Your remarkable and unusual combination of education, experience, knowledge, problems, successes, difficulties and challenges, and your way of looking at and reacting to life, make you extraordinary. You have within you potential competencies and attributes that can enable you to accomplish virtually anything you want in life. Even if you lived for another 100 years, it would not be enough time for you to plumb the depths of your potential. You will never be able to use more than a small part of your inborn abilities. Your main job is to decide which of your talents you're going to exploit and develop to their highest and best possible use right now.

YOUR AREA OF EXCELLENCE

What is your area of excellence? What are you especially good at doing right now? If things continue as they are, what are you likely to be good at in the future—one or two or even five years from today? Is this a marketable skill with a growing demand, or is your field changing in such a way that you are going to have to change as well if you want to keep up with it? Looking into the future, what could be your area of excellence if you were to go to work on yourself and your abilities? What should be your area of excellence if you want to rise to the top of your field, make an excellent living and take complete control of your financial future?

When I was 22, I answered an advertisement for a copywriter for an advertising agency. As it happened, I had failed high-school English, and I really had no idea what a copywriter did. I remember the executive who interviewed me and how nice he was at pointing out that I wasn't at all qualified for the job.

But something happened to me in the course of the interview process. The more I thought about it, the more I thought how much I would like to write advertising. Having been turned down flat during my first interview, I decided to learn more about the field.

I went to the city library and began to check out and read books on advertising and copywriting. Over the next six months, while I worked as a clerk in a department store, I spent many hours devouring them. At the same time, I applied for copywriting jobs to advertising agencies in the city. I started with the smaller agencies first. When they turned me down, I asked them why? What was wrong with my application? What did I need to learn more about? What books would they recommend? And to this day, I remember that virtually everyone I spoke with was helpful to me.

By the end of six months, I had read every book on advertising and copywriting in the city library, and I had applied to every agency in the city, working up from the smallest agency to the very largest in the country. And by the time I had reached that level, I was ready. I was offered jobs as a junior copywriter by both the number-one and number-two agencies in the country. I took the job with the number-one agency and was very successful in a short period of time.

THERE ARE NO LIMITS

The point of this story is that you can become almost anything you need to become, in order to accomplish almost anything you want to accomplish, if you simply decide what it is and then learn what you need to learn. This is such an obvious fact that most people miss it completely.

Some years later, I heard that one could earn a lot of money in real estate development. Again, I went to the library and began checking out and reading all the books I could find on real estate development. At the time, I had no money, no contacts and no knowledge of the industry. But I knew the great secret: I could learn what I needed to learn so that I could do what I wanted to do.

Within 12 months, I had tied up a piece of property with a $100 deposit and a 30-day option. I put together a proposal for a shopping center. I tentatively arranged for two major anchor tenants and several minor tenants that together took up 85 percent of the square footage I had proposed. Then I sold 75 percent of the entire package to a major development company in exchange for the company's putting up all the cash and providing me with the resources and people I needed to manage the construction of the shopping center and the completion of the leasing. Virtually everything that I did I had learned from books written by real estate experts, books on the shelves of the local library.

As you might have noticed, the fields of advertising and copywriting and real estate development are very different. But these experiences, and every business situation I have been in over the years, had one element in common. Success in each area was based on the decision, first, to specialize in that area and, second, to become extremely knowledgeable in that area so that I could do a good job.

In looking at your current and past experiences for an area of specialization, one of the most important questions to ask yourself is, "What activities have been most responsible for my success in life to date?"

How did you get from where you were to where you are today? What talents and abilities seem to come easily to you? What things do you do well that seem to be difficult for most other people? What things do you most enjoy doing? What things do you find most intrinsically motivating? What activities make you happy when you are doing them?

In capitalizing on your strengths, your level of interest, excitement and enthusiasm about the particular job or activity is a key factor. You'll always do best and make the most money in a field that you really enjoy. It will be an area that you like to think about and talk about and read about and learn about. Successful people love what they do, and they can hardly wait to get to it each day. Doing their work makes them happy, and the happier they are, the more enthusiastically they do it, and the better they do it as well.

DIFFERENTIATION IS THE KEY TO SUCCESS IN BUSINESS

In capitalizing on your strengths, the second key to success is differentiation. You must decide what you're going to do to be not only different at doing but also better than your competitors in the field. Remember, you have to be good in only one specific area to move ahead of the pack. And you must decide what that area should be.

SEGMENT YOUR MARKET

The third strategic principle in capitalizing on your strengths is segmentation. You have to look at the marketplace and determine where you can best apply yourself, with your unique talents and abilities, to give yourself the highest possible return on energy expended. What customers, companies, or markets, can best utilize your special talents and offer you the most in terms of financial rewards and future opportunities?

FOCUS AND CONCENTRATION

The final key to personal strategic planning is concentration. Once you have decided the area in which you are going to specialize, how you are going to differentiate yourself, and where in the marketplace you can best apply your strengths, your final job is to concentrate all of your energy on becoming excellent in that specific area. The marketplace only pays extraordinary rewards for extraordinary performance.

In the final analysis, everything that you have done up to now is simply the groundwork for becoming outstanding in your chosen field. When you become very good at doing what people want and need, and are willing to pay for, you begin moving rapidly into the top ranks of the highest paid people everywhere.

And there are no limits.

Branding Small Business

RAYMOND AARON

Branding is an incredibly important tool for creating and building your business. Large companies have been benefiting from branding ever since people first started selling things to other people. Branding made those businesses big.

If you're a small business owner, you probably imagine that small companies are different and don't need branding as much as large companies do. Not true. The truth is small businesses need branding just as much, if not more, than large companies.

Perhaps you've thought about branding, but assumed you'd need millions of dollars to do it properly, or that branding is just the same thing as marketing. Nothing could be further from the truth.

Marketing is the engine of your company's success. Branding is the fuel in that engine.

In the old days, salespeople were a big part of the selling process. They recommended one product over another and laid out the reasons why it was better. Salespeople had credibility because they knew about all the products, and customers often took the advice they had to offer.

Today, consumers control the buying process. They shop in big box stores, super-sized supermarkets, and over the Internet—where there are no salespeople. Buyers now get online and gather information beforehand. They learn about all the products available and look to see if there really is any difference between them. Consumers also read reviews and check social media to see if both the company and the product are reputable. In other words, they want to know what the brand is all about.

The way of commerce used to be: "Nothing happens till something is sold." Today it's: "Nothing happens till something is branded!"

DEFINING A BRAND

A brand is a proper name that stands for something. It lives in the consumer's mind, has positive or negative characteristics, and invokes a feeling or an image. In short, it's a person's perception of a product or a company.

When all goes well, consumers associate the same characteristics with a brand that the company talks about in its advertising, public relations, marketing and sales materials. Of course, when a product doesn't live up to what the company says about it, the brand gets a bad reputation. On the other hand, if a product or service over-delivers on the promises made, the brand can become a superstar.

RECOGNIZING BRANDING AND ITS CHARACTERISTICS

Branding is the science and art of making something that isn't unique, unique. Branding in the marketplace is the same as branding on a ranch. On a ranch, ranchers use branding to differentiate their cattle from every other rancher's cattle (because all cattle look pretty much the same). In the marketplace, branding is what makes a product stand out in a crowd of similar products. The right branding gets you noticed, remembered, and sold—or perhaps I should say bought, because today it is all about buying, not selling.

There are four main characteristics of branding that make it an integral part of the marketing and purchasing process:

1. **Branding makes you trustworthy and known.** Branding makes a product more special than other products. With branding, a normal, everyday product has a personality, and a first and last name, and people know who you are.

    In today's marketplace, most products are, more or less, just like their competition. Toilet paper is toilet paper, milk is milk, and a grocery store by any other name is still a grocery store.

    However, branding takes a product and makes it unique. For example, high-quality drinking water is available from just about every tap in the

Western world and it's free, but people pay good money for it when it comes in a bottle. Branding takes bottled water and makes Evian.

Furthermore, every aspect of your brand gives potential customers a feeling or comfort level that they associate with you. The more powerful and positive that feeling is, the more easily and more frequently they will want to do business with you and, indeed, will do business with you.

2. **Branding differentiates you from others.** Strong branding makes you better than your competition, and makes your product name memorable and easy to remember. Even if your product is absolutely the same as every other product like it, branding makes it special. Branding makes it the first product a consumer thinks about when deciding to make a purchase.

   Branding also makes a product seem popular. Everyone knows about it, which implicitly says people like it. And, if people like it, it must be good.

3. **Branding makes you worth more money.** The stronger your branding is, the more likely people are willing to spend that little bit extra because they believe you, your product, your service, or your business are worth it. They may say they won't, but they will. They do it all the time.

   For example, a one-pound box of Godiva chocolates costs about $40; the same weight of Hershey's Kisses costs about $4. The quality of the chocolate isn't 10 times greater. The reason people buy Godiva is that the brand Godiva means "gift" whereas the brand Hershey means "snack." Gifts obviously cost more than snacks.

4. **Branding pre-sells your product.** In the buying age, people most often make the decision on which products to pick up before they walk into the store. The stronger the branding, the more likely people are to think

in terms of your product rather than the product category. For example, people are as likely, maybe even more likely, to add Hellmann's to the shopping list as they are to write down simply mayo. The same is true for soda, ketchup, and many other products with successful, strong branding.

Plus, as soon as a shopper gets to the shelf, branding can provide a quick reminder of what products to grab in a few ways:

- An icon or logo
- A specific color
- An audio icon

BRANDING IN A SMALL BUSINESS

Big companies spend millions of dollars on advertising, marketing, and public relations (PR) to build recognition of a new product name. They get their selling messages out to the public using television, radio, magazines, and the Internet. They can even throw money at damage control when necessary. The strategies for branding are the same in a small business, but the scale, costs, and a few of the tactics change.

Make your brand name work harder

The name of a small business can mean everything in terms of branding. Your brand name needs to work harder for your business than you do. It's the first thing a prospective customer sees, and it is how they will remember you. A brand name has to be memorable when spoken, and focused in its meaning. If the name doesn't represent what consumers believe about a product and the company that makes it, then that brand will fail.

In building your product's reputation and image, less is often significantly more. Make sure the name you choose immediately gives a sense of what you do.

Large corporations have millions of dollars to take a meaningless brand name and make it stand for something. Small businesses don't, so use words that really mean something. Strive for something interesting and be right on point. You don't need to be boring.

Plumbers, for example, would do well setting themselves apart with names like "The On-Time Plumber" or "24/7 Plumbing." The same is true for electricians, IT providers, or even marketing consultants. Plenty of other types of business are so general in nature they just don't work hard enough in a business or product name.

Even the playing field: The Net

The Internet has leveled the playing field for small businesses like nothing else. You can use the Internet in several ways to market your brand:

> Website: Developing and maintaining a website is easier than ever. Anyone can find your business regardless of its size.

> Social Media: Facebook, Instagram, LinkedIn, YouTube and Twitter can promote your brand in a cost-effective manner.

BUILDING YOUR BRAND WITH THE BRANDING LADDER

Even if you do everything perfectly the first time (and I don't know anyone who does), branding takes time. How much time isn't just up to you, but you can speed things along by understanding the different levels of branding, as well as the business and marketing strategies that can get you to the top.

Introducing the Branding Ladder

Moving through the levels of branding is like climbing a ladder to the top of the marketplace. The Branding Ladder has five distinct rungs, and unlike stairs, you can't take them two at a time. You have to take them in order, and some businesses spend more time on each rung than others.

You can also think of the Branding Ladder in terms of a scale from zero to 10. Everyone starts at zero. If you properly climb the ladder, you can end up at 12 out of 10. The Branding Ladder below shows a special rung at the top of the ladder that can take your business over the top. The following section explains the Branding Ladder and how your small business can move up it.

THE BRANDING LADDER	
Brand Advocacy	12/10
Brand Insistence	10/10
Brand Preference	3/10
Brand Awareness	1/10
Brand Absence	0/10

Rung 1: Living in the void. Your business, in fact every business, starts at the bottom rung, which is called brand absence, meaning you have no brand whatsoever except your own name. On a scale of one to 10, brand absence is,

of course, zero. That's the worst place to live and obviously the most difficult entrepreneurially. The good news is that the only way is up.

Ninety-seven percent of businesses live on this rung of the Branding Ladder. They earn far less than they want to earn, far less than they should earn, and far less than they would earn if they did exactly the same work under a real brand.

Rung 2: Achieving awareness. Brand awareness is a good first step up the ladder to the second rung. Actually, it's really good, especially because 97 percent of businesses never get there. You want people to be aware of you. When person A speaks to person B and says, "Have you heard of "The 24/7 Plumber?" You want the answer to be "yes."

On that scale of one to 10, however, brand awareness is only a one. It's better than nothing, but not that much better. Although people know of your brand, being aware doesn't mean that they are interested in buying it. Coca-Cola drinkers know about Pepsi, but they don't drink it.

Rung 3: Becoming the preferred brand. Getting to the third rung, brand preference, is definitely a real step up. This rung means that people prefer to use your product or service rather than that of your competition. They believe there is a real difference between you and others, and you're their first choice. This rung is a crucial branding stage for parity products, such as bottled water and breakfast cereals, not to mention plumbers, electricians, lawyers, and all the others. Brand preference is clearly better than brand awareness, but it's less than halfway up the ladder.

Car rental companies represent a perfect example of why brand preference may not be enough. When someone lands at an airport and needs to rent a car on the spot, he or she may go straight to the preferred rental counter. If that company has a car available, it's a sale. However, if all the cars for that company have been rented, the person will move to the next rental kiosk without much thought, because one rental car is just as good as another.

Exerting brand preference needs to be easy and convenient!

If all you have is brand preference, your business is on shaky ground and you can lose business for the feeblest of reasons. Very few people go to a second or third supermarket just to find their favorite brand of bottled water. Similarly, a shopper may prefer one store over another, but if both stores sell the same products, he or she will often go to the closest store even if it is not the better liked one. The reason for staying nearby does not need to be a dramatic one—the shopper may simply be tired, on a tight schedule, or not in the mood to travel.

Rung 4: Making it you and only you. When your customers are so committed to your product or service that they won't accept a substitute, you have reached the fourth rung of the Branding Ladder. All companies strive to reach this place, called brand insistence.

Brand insistence means that someone's experience with a product in terms of performance, durability, customer service, and image has been sufficiently exceptional. As a result, the product has earned an incredible level of loyalty. If the product isn't available where the customer is, he or she will literally not buy something else. Rather, the person will look for the preferred product elsewhere. Can you imagine what a fabulous place this is for a company to be? Brand insistence is the best of the best, the perfect 10 out of 10, the whole ball of wax.

Apple is a perfect example of brand insistence. Apple users don't just think, they know in their heads and hearts, that anything made by Apple is technologically-advanced, user-friendly, and just all-around superior.

Committed to everything Apple, Mac users won't even entertain the thought that a PC may have positive attributes.

Apple people love everything about their Macs, iPads, iPhones, the Mac stores, and all those apps. When the company introduces a new product, many of its brand-insistent fans actually wait in line overnight to be one of the first to have it. Steve Jobs is one of their idols.

Unfortunately, you can lose brand insistence much more quickly than you can achieve it. Brand-insistent customers have such high expectations that they can be disillusioned or disappointed by just one bad product experience. You also have to consistently reinforce the positives because insistence can fade over time. Even someone who has bought and re-bought a specific brand of car for the last 20 years can decide it's just time for a change. That's how fickle the world is.

At 10 out of 10, brand insistence may seem like the top rung of the ladder, but it's not. One rung is actually better, and it involves getting your brand-insistent customers to keep polishing your brand for you.

Rung 5: Getting customers to do the work for you. Brand advocacy is the highest rung on the ladder. It's better than 10 out of 10 because you have customers who are so happy with your product that they want everyone to know about it and use it. Think of them as uber-fans. Not only do they recommend you to friends and family, they also practically shout your praises from the rooftops, interrupt conversations among strangers to give their opinion, and tell everyone they meet how fantastic you are. Most companies can only aspire to this level of customer satisfaction. Apple is one of the few large corporations in recent history that has brand advocates all over the world.

Brand advocacy does the following five extraordinary things for your company.

Brand Advocacy

1. **Provides a level of visibility that you couldn't pay for if you tried.** Brand advocates are so enthusiastic they talk about you all the time and reach people in ways general media and public relations can't. You get great visibility because they make sure people actually listen.

2. **Delivers free advertising and public relations.** Companies love the extra super-positive messaging, all for free.

3. **Affords a level of credibility that literally can't be bought.** Brand advocates are more than just walking testimonials. They are living proof that you are the best.

4. **Provides pre-sold prospective customers.** Advocate recommendations carry so much weight that they are worth much more than plain referrals. They deliver customers ready and committed to purchasing your product or service.

5. **Increases profits exponentially.** Brand advocates are money-making machines for your business because they increase sales and decrease marketing costs.

For these reasons, brand advocacy is 12 out of 10!!

BRANDING YOURSELF: HOW TO DO SO IN FOUR EASY WAYS

If you're interested in branding your product or company, you may not be sure where to begin. The good news: I'm here to help.

You can brand in many ways, but here I pare it down to four ways to help you start:

1. **Branding by association.** This way involves hanging out with and being seen with people who are very much higher than you in your particular niche.

2. **Branding by achievement.** This way repurposes your previous achievements.

3. **Branding by testimonial.** This way makes use of the testimonials that you receive but have likely never used.

4. **Branding by WOW.** A WOW is the pleasantly unexpected, the equivalent of going the extra mile. The easiest and most certain way to WOW people is to tell them that you've written a book. To discover how you can write a book, go to www.BrandingSmallBusinessForDummies.com.

What the World Needs Now

How to Cultivate More Love in Your Life and Change the World

ANGELA GOLDEN BRYAN

"What the world needs now is love, sweet love
It's the only thing that there's just too little of
What the world needs now is love, sweet love,
No not just for some but for everyone..."

- Jackie DeShannon

Sometimes it may seem like the world is filled with negativity and chaos. No matter who you are or where you live, the world around you can change overnight. Perhaps it was already evolving slowly, but you were too busy to notice or didn't want to acknowledge it. When the world seems to be spinning out of control, remember that, despite the anxiety, frustration, and negativity, we all have the choice as to how we will respond to it. You may not be able to control the world around you, but you can manage your thoughts better. My first introduction to this life-changing truth occurred in high school when I read Viktor Frankl's groundbreaking book, "Man's Search for Meaning." Frankl was imprisoned in a concentration camp during WWII and experienced daily physical, verbal, and emotional abuse. Although he faced uncertainty, and even death, during that horrific time, he survived by realizing he still had control over his thoughts. Frankl developed techniques that helped him choose positive thoughts over negative ones. After reading this compelling book, it was clear to me that choosing to discipline my mind, and not have it controlled by outward circumstances, was an essential key to finding personal happiness, joy, and fulfillment.

THE IMPORTANCE OF OUR THOUGHTS IN TIMES OF CRISIS

While I'm writing this, we are living through an unprecedented time in modern history. The world is in the throes of the COVID -19 pandemic and there are worldwide anti-racist protests calling for systemic change. On the occasions that I tune into the media, scenes of growing fear, hatred, rage, and anxiety confront me. Misinformation is also spreading, and much of it adds to the feeling of chaos and despair for many. What I know to be true is that what we think controls our feelings and emotions, which leads to our actions. Our actions include how we interact with others, as well as ourselves.

Some daily tools that help me to maintain healthy thoughts are praying, reading Scripture, and saying affirmations. When I use the word "affirmation," I am referring to an encouraging statement, based on God's truth and how he sees me and my circumstances. For example, if I'm feeling fearful and lonely, I might repeat the following affirmation: "God is always with me, he gives me courage." I based this affirmation on the Bible verse: "Be strong and courageous. Do not be afraid or terrified because of them, for the Lord your God goes with you; he will never leave you nor forsake you." (NIV, Deuteronomy 31:6) When I habitually practice these strategies, I tend to have more positive thoughts, feel better about myself, others, and life, and my actions are more conducive to health. This practice has come in handy when confronted by simple tasks that now have the capacity to be a bit stressful due to the current events.

One example is venturing out to buy groceries. Once, after enjoying a car ride filled with upbeat songs and affirmations, I entered the market feeling energized and joy-filled. However, I noticed that the workers weren't their usual cheerful selves. Instead, they seemed subdued and did not engage in their customary "small talk." Before I knew what was happening, I burst into song. The song that came to me was a hit from many years ago: "What the world needs now is love, sweet love. It's the only thing that there's just too little of…" I wasn't even through a third of the song when a few people joined in, and together we sang this happy tune about love being "the only thing that there's just too little of." It felt like a scene out of a Broadway musical. We laughed and smiled, knowing we had brightened the atmosphere.

Reflecting on my experience while driving home, I felt grateful to be part of such a fun and loving experience. (And with strangers no less!) However, a line from the song continued to loop through my mind "… it's the only thing that there's just too little of." Was it true? Is there a love shortage? Are people hoarding love as opposed to giving it away? Are people selling their love to the highest bidder?

"What the world needs now is love…" Truer words have never been spoken. The world is hurting and needs love; however, I refuse to believe that there isn't enough love to go around. I think that perhaps we've forgotten how to love. I encourage you to find love within yourself and learn how to cultivate and share it. Let's start with those closest and spread our love to the world, one person at a time. I believe in your capacity to love and look forward to being a part of your "love journey." Let's examine what love is, take a look at the part forgiveness plays, and step onto a clearer path back to LOVE.

HOW DO WE DEFINE LOVE?

We all use the word "love" in our everyday life. You may express it to someone by saying, "I love you" or exclaim that you "love" something. But have you ever stopped and asked yourself how you'd define love? Curious, I went online and searched: "What is the best definition of love?" The following answers came up in my search: "The most spectacular, indescribable, deep euphoric feeling for someone; love is an incredibly powerful word; love is unconditional affection with no limits or conditions; (love is) when you trust the other with your life and when you would do anything for each other."

Next, I sought an answer from the Bible. Here is 1 Corinthians' description: "Love is patient, love is kind. It does not envy, it does not boast; it is not proud. It does not dishonor others, it is not self-seeking, it is not easily angered, it keeps no record of wrongs. Love does not delight in evil but rejoices with the truth. It always protects, always trusts, always hopes, always perseveres." (NIV, 1 Corinthians 13:4-7)

Both online and in the Bible, love is the grand undertaking. Words such as "no limits and conditions" as well as "always," may create a feeling of immense pressure around what love is. I don't know that I can "always" love, or love without "limits and conditions," but I do believe it is worth trying! Perhaps the best place to start is to examine what love is not.

WHAT LOVE IS NOT

I believe that all of us are familiar with the face of "unloving." Unloving is the opposite of love, even though some try to pass it off as love. I have seen my fair share of it, and have acted in unloving ways on more than one occasion. Some prime examples are controlling others, manipulation, jealousy, obsession, lack of boundaries, and codependency. Love goes beyond romantic relationships and includes all manner of partnerships and alliances (including the one you have with yourself). Based on 1 Corinthians 13:4-7, we see that love does not: encourage envy, dishonor others, keep a record of wrongs, or delight in evil. We also understand that love is not: proud, self-seeking, or easily angered. All of the actions and states of being mentioned above stem from fear and show us what the opposite of love is. To move towards being a more loving person, we must eliminate these unloving behaviors. The process may be challenging, and you may come up against years of negative thought patterns. However, just imagine the rewards you will reap by doing this work!

The laws of physics tell us that nature abhors a void, so if a vacuum exists, something will fill it. If we are not intentional about what fills a space, something less than desirable may "sneak" in and fill it. This law is seen in nature and is no less visible in our personal lives. I do not have what some call a "green thumb;" however, I have grown potted herbs over the years. On more than one occasion, I've purchased pots, soil, and seeds, began the process, only to get side tracked. After putting dirt in a container, I got distracted and left it untended for a few days. When I finally came back, weeds were growing out of the pots. I had not planted "weed" seeds, but they found their way into my untended soil! So it is in life; weeds of negativity spring up without our intentionally planting them. If you want love to fill the void, it is essential to be intentional about "planting" seeds of love. Often, we must first uproot weeds before we can replace them with love. To choose love, we must recognize love. If we don't know what love looks like, we may settle for weeds of negativity, which grow into unhealthy thoughts, emotions, and finally, behaviors.

WHAT IS LOVE?

If you define what love is and make it personal, you will have the power to invite more of it into your life. Referring back to 1 Corinthians 13:4-7, love is: patient and kind, and it protects, trusts, hopes, perseveres, and rejoices with the truth. These loving qualities will be most welcome into your life when you are willing to release fear, greed, envy, competition, expectation, judgment, and a critical spirit. As we release the non-supportive and negative thoughts, emotions, and actions, we learn to love ourselves and others more. You will find that, every time you are willing to let something go, you will open yourself up to new possibilities. When you release the expectation that you, or others, need to be perfect, you will cultivate more patience. When you treat others as you would like to be treated, you are more kind and, in turn, invite more kindness into your life. When you release the fear of rejection, abandonment, and being cheated, you will trust more. All these actions will bring more love into your life because these positive actions are ways that we love. We find the strength to make these changes in God. By trusting God, you will persevere, and love will flourish in your life.

PERSONALIZED LOVE

While it's helpful to discuss what love is or is not, it is also essential to keep in mind that love looks different based on each person's personality. The truth that "love is kind" may mean giving a hug to the personality type that is motivated by relationships. In contrast, it may mean contributing to household chores for the goal-oriented personality type. In my workshops, I help people discover their unique personality blends, which brings clarity to how they see themselves and others. This clarity takes the "puzzle" out of relationships and frees individuals to love on a personal, authentic level. This simple process can be life-changing.

The starting point is understanding that everyone is not like you, and you're not like anyone else. From this healthy model of personality, we also understand that being different is not bad; it's just different. With this in mind, we know that love will look and feel different for each individual. Everyone is unique, so it makes sense that giving and receiving love may not look the same to those around you.

I have taught personality profiles to couples, teens, corporate teams, and women's groups for better understanding relationships. It is exciting to see lightbulbs go off in people's minds as they come to understand why they have experienced a feeling of disconnect in particular relationships, be it at work, home, houses of worship, or school. Everyone expresses and receives love in unique ways, which may be different from our own. It is of great value to understand your personality blend so that you will have more empowered relationships with everyone. Contact me directly at AngelaGoldenBryan.com to set up a free consultation to see if my "Solving Your People Puzzles" workshop is right for you, your family, or business.

RETURNING TO LOVE

When returning to love, you must first become aware of behaviors that block you from love. One of my mentors, Dr. Robert Rohm, says, "We cannot beware of something until we are first aware of it." It makes sense, doesn't it?

Once you are aware of the behaviors keeping you from love, the next step is to release these behaviors. As previously mentioned in 1 Corinthians 13:4-7, negative mindsets such as envy or being easily angered keep us from love. To release the fears associated with competition, sense of lack, judgment, manipulation, control, unforgiveness, and revenge, we must see ourselves as God sees us. Seeing ourselves as God sees us, as well as seeing others as God sees them, is a vital part of the path to love. When we understand that God made us in His image and that we each have a purpose for being here, we come closer to learning how to love more deeply.

HOW GOD FEELS ABOUT YOU AND LOVE

"The mountains and hills may crumble, but my love for you will never end." (GNT, Isaiah 54:10) When you ground yourself in God's love, you set yourself up to love others, even in challenging times. It's easier to be a loving person when you understand and remember why God loves you. Feeling God's love will remove fears, and as previously mentioned, there is more room for love when there is less fear in your life. Pastor Rick Warren gave some crucial reminders of what God thinks of us in one of his daily devotionals. Here are a few of my favorites that help me remember why and how to love.

God Accepts You as You Are:

"Jesus . . . made us acceptable to God." (CEV, Titus 3:7) No matter what you've done or what you do, by dying on the cross, Jesus has made us entirely justifiable to God. We are "right" with God. We spend a lot of time trying to gain the acceptance of others, but what matters is that you are already accepted fully by God.

God Loves You Unconditionally:

God doesn't say, "I love you if . . ." or "I love you because . . ." He says, "I love you—period!" You can't make God stop loving you, because his love is not based on what you do but on who he is. God's reassurance of this truth states: "The mountains and hills may crumble, but my love for you will never end." (GNT, Isaiah 54:10)

God Wholeheartedly Forgives You:

God doesn't rehearse your sins; he releases them because they are done and over with. Jesus died on the cross and gave his life as a sacrifice for your sins. Jesus' sacrificial death means that you are forgiven when you accept the gift of forgiveness from God. Romans 8:1 puts it this way: "There is no condemnation for those who belong to Christ Jesus." (NLT)

You're Valuable in God's Sight:

You are a child of God and "have been bought and paid for by Christ" (TLB,

1 Corinthians 7:23) Jesus Christ paid for your life by offering his own life. The price that someone is willing to pay for something is often indicative of how valuable it is. Jesus' life is the highest price ever paid – that makes you priceless!

Remember that it is not about what you or others think about yourself; it is about what God thinks about you.

FORGIVENESS

One of the main blocks to cultivating more love in your life is holding on to resentment and not being able to forgive. Forgiveness is critical in bringing joy and growth to your life. What you must realize is that not being able to forgive will harm you more than the offender. I've heard it said many times, and I'll repeat it here: Holding on to resentment is like drinking poison and expecting the other person to die!

Forgiveness is when we choose to let go of feelings of resentment or anger against another when we feel hurt, rejected, or treated poorly by them. We must forgive, whether we believe the other person deserves it or not. Remember that when you forgive, it doesn't mean you condone their behavior. It also doesn't mean that you have to maintain a relationship with them, especially if they are a threat to your safety and wellbeing. When you forgive, you follow God's example because he forgave you.

When you don't forgive others, you affect your emotional and physical wellbeing, often without realizing it. Many of us have seen the pain and suffering that unforgiveness brings the unforgiving individual. I have also experienced this pain, and so it is with love and understanding that I encourage you to forgive and make space for love. Your health and happiness depend on it. Learning to forgive is crucial for your wellbeing!

STEPS TO FORGIVENESS

Although I present several steps to forgiveness in this chapter, I encourage you to embrace the fact that forgiveness is a process and may have a timeline of its own, regardless of how sincere you are. The desire to forgive may be there, yet you might still feel that "niggling" feeling in your stomach. Anger, resentment, and even rage may threaten to rise to the surface. If this happens, don't give up. Keep at it until there isn't a "knee-jerk" response to the individual you are seeking to forgive. Repeat the steps, pray for God to help you forgive, and be patient with yourself. You will get there if that is your desire, and you are taking the active steps towards forgiveness.

Revisit the Occasion of "Offense": Be willing to think about the events that led to your feeling hurt or resentful. Think about your past reaction as well as how you currently feel. How has it affected your mind, mood, or actions?

Role Play: Imagine how the other person may have felt or what they may have been thinking. When you do this, you are exercising empathy. Empathy is invaluable when going through the process of forgiveness. Being mindful of other people's stories and histories can help you connect with the bigger picture, and discover possible reasons why the conflict has arisen. It may not be 100% their fault. Remember that no one is perfect, including yourself.

Release Attachment to the End Result: When going through the process of forgiveness, do not be attached to a specific outcome or action from the other person. For example, although you desire it, apologies or reconciliations may not occur between you and the person you are working on forgiving.

Be Intentional by Choosing to Forgive: Choosing to forgive another is one of the most liberating decisions you can make. It doesn't have to occur in a conversation; it can be as simple as writing about it in a journal or even talking to someone you trust.

Include Yourself: Forgiving yourself is as crucial as forgiving others. All of us have had moments in our lives that we are not proud of, and we've all made mistakes. It is just as essential to go through the forgiveness process with yourself so that you can let go of resentment and anger, thereby allowing more room for love.

FILLING YOUR LIFE WITH LOVE

"Keep company with him and learn a life of love. Observe how Christ loved us. His love was not cautious but extravagant. He didn't love to get something from us but to give everything of himself to us. Love like that." (MSG, Ephesians 5:2)

Becoming a loving person will not happen overnight. It is a process, but a worthwhile one that will change you and your relationships forever. I have followed Joyce Meyer's teachings for years, and I admire her authentic teachings on love. Without shame for her failures, she shares her love journey in a way that only she can do. Here are some practical tips on where to start:

- Learn how mature love acts and responds by reflecting God's word.

- Dedicate the first 10 minutes of your day to reflect on love and ask for God's help.

- Memorize Scripture focusing on love so that you can easily refer to it in trying times.

- Love is a muscle that needs strengthening, so practice!

- Join a small group of people that are dedicated to filling their life with more love.

As I continue to apply these teachings to my life, my capacity to love increases. Each day that I commit to working on my "love walk," I get better. I invite you to do the same.

LOVE IS A SKILL

When developing a new skill, you first have to decide that you want to learn. After that decision you must be willing to dedicate your time to developing that skill. Love is a skill that you can develop and grow. It's not fair to expect that you will be a master at loving right away. But know that you can be a better lover than you are now. Practicing love and getting better at it is what God wants of you. God wants you to be a master when it comes to love! Like any new skill, the growth curve may feel awkward, and you may encounter many setbacks on your path to mastery. But setbacks are never a reason to give up, because every master was once a disaster! Trust that you will gain confidence, and with God on your side, you will have the power to become an expert at love.

I can only write based on my experience and I come to you knowing that God is my Father; Jesus is his Son, and he died for my sins; and that the Holy Spirit empowers and comforts me. This is the foundational truth upon which this chapter is written. If you don't have a personal relationship with Jesus, please join me by saying this simple, yet life-changing prayer:

Dear Heavenly Father,

I know that I am not perfect and have missed the mark. I have sinned and I am sorry and ask for your forgiveness. I believe Jesus died on the cross and that he rose from the dead, and is alive today. I surrender and ask Jesus to be my Savior and live in my heart and my life. I thank you for accepting me just as I am, and for loving me enough to not let me stay this way. I believe you are now my Savior and that the Holy Spirit lives in me. Thank you, Father. Amen.

For more inspiration, healthy lifestyle tips, and fun, connect with me online. I look forward to journeying with you, one love-step at a time, as we live our God-given purpose together!

AngelaGoldenBryan.com
www.instagram.com/AngelaGoldenBryan
youtube.com/c/AngelaGoldenBryan

The Mindset of Success

ANNA GRIFFIN

My mother said something to me once that has stuck in my mind ever since, and that is, "Conviction and comfort don't live in the same block." If you want your life to be fulfilling and continually reach your goals and dreams, then there are going to be times of discomfort and overcoming fear.

When I started writing this chapter, I was completely filled with fear, uncertainty, and confusion. I guess it was fear of having my thoughts heard, and thinking, "Who am I to say all this?" or "What will others say?" These types of thoughts and questions often accompany us in moments when we least want it or expect it. "Am I strong enough?" "Am I going to be accepted and will I fit in?" are our common thoughts. But quickly enough I thought to myself, "Well, what's the worst thing that is going to happen?" I set myself back on track to have the right mindset and to think of the many exceptional leaders I have been fortunate to work for throughout my career and travels.

I've made it my mission to understand their exceptional attributes, which served them in moments of fear and self-doubt. But it is not always about the tools that are being used, the business models or the frameworks. Often, it is more about their mindset and leadership and what kind of people we become in their presence.

Living in many countries and getting to know different cultures, from the West to the East, I have had the privilege to better understand what makes a person successful, happy, and someone you would want to follow as a business leader, or because of their humble yet inspiring way of life.

So, I searched, and continue to search, for inspiration from them and the application of their mindsets, their extreme discipline, and their right habits in real life and workplace. The understanding of how we can be enemies to ourselves when it comes to fulfillment and achieving what we really desire in life prompted me to share and get it all out. Not only that, it was a true journey into myself that gave me clarity about what will come next.

In my book, Reimagine the Possible, I go into details of the attributes and tools of success and happiness, and how to apply them to your life. In this chapter, I am going to highlight some of them, to get you started on your road of possibilities.

THE WILL TO CHANGE

*"It isn't the mountain ahead to climb that wears you down.
It's the pebbles in your shoes."*
- Muhammad Ali

There are a few distinct features that set successful people apart from those who fail. It's not always the talent or number of titles they have behind their name, but it's their mindset and the few things they do differently than majority of us. First, they are able to develop strong and fulfilling relationships, alliances, and connections that will help them build their business, create their success, and open the doors to potential opportunities.

Second, they don't procrastinate, but act on their plan, and the things they passionately want to do. Often, what most people do is wait until the perfect time comes and put things off till tomorrow that they should do today; e.g. "I'll start my new online business when I get more support from my partner or the economy is better," or "I will create a better website for my business once my kids get out of the house." "I will start taking care of myself later." There is always a 'but' that we keep saying to ourselves.

Third, they don't give up, they are persistent, and they keep going with their plan. They understand that success will not be achieved instantaneously. How often do we start something but never finish it because it gets too tough, too time-consuming, or too overwhelming? If we face those few things and persevere, I believe, we might be quite successful and happy in our professional and personal lives.

Of course, the journey is never easy. Success doesn't happen overnight. It will take time, but if you believe in your abilities, have the right mindset and perseverance, and above all work hard, you will get there. The hard work is not only related to achieving your professional or career goals. It is also hard work on yourself, your beliefs, fears, and habits, all of which this chapter will discuss.

What's important is not what you will or will not do, or whether you will or will not change. It is whether you have the will to change – to plan and act so that you can start doing the things that you know you should.

NO SMOOTH MOUNTAIN

We keep dreaming about how one day we could reach our full potential, and the goals we always wanted to get to. But we often don't realize that we are as capable of genius as the most successful people in the world. We look at people like Oprah, Steve Jobs, and Richard Branson, and think, "If I only had their ideas, their genius", or "They are so lucky." You ask yourself, "How can I find my true purpose and passion in life? Why can't I never figure out how to be successful and happy like them?" But nobody, and especially the most successful in the world, thinks they are special until they make themselves special.

Nobody starts their business knowing that they will instantly become multi-billionaires. The difference starts with their mindset, the plan they have, and the actions they take. What sets the successful people apart from the less successful ones is that they do what most people don't want to do or are hesitant to do. Perhaps they hesitate because they are terrified of the unknown or they believe they are too busy, that it's beyond their capabilities, or maybe people around them would say it's not possible, that it is out of their reach and they will never get there. The other group, the fulfilled ones, listen to themselves and pursue their dreams, no matter the obstacles, and they ignore the naysayers.

Will you struggle? Will it be hard? Yes. You may fall many times, but who is counting? The best successes are made from failures. In fact, I don't believe there are failures, only lessons learned. You must remember that no single mountain is smooth. If you want to get to the top, there are sharp ridges that must be stepped over. There will be times that will be stressful, and you might be disappointed and discouraged.

FEAR

"No person can be confronted with a difficulty which has not the strength to meet and subdue. Every difficulty can be overcome if rightly dealt with. Anxiety is, therefore, unnecessary. The task which cannot be overcome ceases to be a difficulty and becomes impossibility and there's only one way of dealing with an impossibility, namely to submit to it."
- Byways of Blessedness, James Allen

When we are confronted with difficulties, over time they create a great amount of anxiety. We may be faced with decisions that have long-term ramifications for our life or career and would affect not only us, but also those close to us. Those are decisions that we would rather not have to make. They just make us want to pull a blanket over our head and wish they would disappear together with the light that disappears once the same blanket covers our hair.

The question that I started to ask myself was, "Where are my fears coming from and why am I allowing them to stop me from moving forward?

James Allen's words in the quote are very profound, and the essence is that there is no problem that cannot be resolved. I like to think about it in this way: if an issue that I am facing can be resolved with an action, then I don't have an issue. It is simply something that needs to be resolved and is just something that we encounter in our lives or at work. So, remember, if an issue can be solved with action, then it is not an issue.

This has been my approach to any challenge that has been placed in front of me throughout my career and life. I treat it like something exciting to resolve and put my best effort into coming up with the best solution.

A substantial body of research shows that our brain can't actually differentiate physical fear (e.g. car crash) from emotional fear (e.g. being afraid of a spider). In addition, research also shows that in the brain fear and excitement are caused by the same neurochemical signals, i.e. cortisol and norepinephrine. Steven Kotler talks about this at length in his research, and shows that fear and flow (or the peak performance) are at the opposite sides of the same spectrum. They are both caused by the same neurochemical reaction in the brain, initiated by cortisol and norepinephrine.

Successful people learn to reframe the fear and use it as their compass; if something that they want to do produces some level of fear, then this is exactly what they will do. They will do what scares them the most, what feels uncomfortable. Only by doing this will they be able to push their boundaries, and this will give them the progress and growth needed to accomplish what they want. Below are some ways that help to acknowledge and reframe fear:

1. Acknowledge the changes that are happening and how they are affecting you – how does the event make you feel?

2. Ask 'Do I have enough information and facts to support my fear?'

3. Reframe the context. Say to yourself that you are excited about the event. This will switch your brain from feeling anxious and nervous to feeling excited and positive (no danger is coming).

4. What's the payoff? What is the price that I will pay if I don't reframe and stay in the state of fear, which will negatively impact my performance and future prospects? What will my career look like?

You must remember that we fear and are anxious about things that we create in our minds and imagine that they may happen to us. We think that external forces create our anxiety or fear and we only respond to those events. But our response to any situation, however bad it may be, is our choice and the result of our thoughts and beliefs.

I always like to remind myself that most things that we imagine out of fear never happen. Mark Twain famously once said, "I have lived a long life and had many fears, most of which never happened."

MASTER THE MINDSET

"Beliefs have the power to create and power to destroy," as Tony Robbins, the motivational speaker and life coach, said. You see, our beliefs about the events around us or what happens to us are what shaped us into who we are today and who we will become tomorrow. But the fact is that many of us grew up around people who inadvertently passed on their limiting beliefs to us, and we might have been conditioned to the negative thinking that they grew up with. But remember, our past doesn't define us and there is no point in playing the blame game with them for passing their limiting beliefs onto you.

Research tells us that our thoughts and responses are shaped by our subconscious mind and they are aligned to the paradigms that we grew up with. For example, you might have had people in your life who constantly told you, "Since you haven't done it till now, you are just not cut out for it." This environment conditioned your thoughts and created paradigms in your subconscious mind. You start creating excuses without even realizing it, and eventually you will quit pursuing your dream.

If you want to have a successful career or follow your dreams, you need to evaluate whether your own mind is your biggest enemy and if you are acting according to old paradigms that shaped your thoughts, and hence your decisions, actions, and results. If so, a change is needed.

First, you will need to decide that you want to change your paradigm. Change is never easy, but once you realize that some of your old patterns, actions, and decisions are a result of the environment you were raised in or are surrounded by now, then you will see how this impacts your current life. I always like to remind myself of something that Wayne Dyer, American philosopher and author, said: "When you change the way you look at things, things that you look at change." Don't make yourself a victim of the circumstances surrounding you, or those that you cannot control.

Our life, career, and relationships are a reflection of the approach we take towards them. We are fully responsible for how things turn out for us – whether we are successful or not, have savings, a fulfilled relationship at home, a loving family, and so on. Let's say, your team is not producing the results you wish, or your business is not going well. Perhaps you are not paying attention to the relationships within your team and let them just run, or maybe the decisions you made were not the right ones. We are the only ones that have the power to take responsibility for the change we are looking for. We waste our most finite resource, time, to find external reasons that cause change. But once we shift this mindset, our life, career, and relationships will start getting into gear.

So, whatever we've learned and experienced in the past, we've accepted it as a truth at an unconscious level, and now it doesn't matter if what we've learned is correct or not, we still accept it as a truth. These are the 'life's apps' that we created for each aspect of our life – you have an app for everything that gives you a point of reference to go back to and check out how it should be done. I've realized over the years how this led to developing unconscious behaviors and habits in me.

"The beliefs that you have about yourself and your abilities are not facts. They are your tightly held opinions. In other words, it's not primarily about your ability. It's what you believe about your ability that shapes your potential success."
- Dr. Stan Beecham, Elite Minds

I also realized how often my belief system was empowering me or, unfortunately, disempowering me. You can take any experience in your life and make it into a very meaningful and empowering capability. Or it can be the opposite; your experiences and beliefs can be limiting you. You can take a painful experience and make it into powerful and motivating strength that will empower you to do anything you dreamt of.

There are a few simple ways that can help you work on your old paradigm and create change. I have done this myself, and it helped me realize how my own old conditioning was affecting my life, career, and relationships.

- Ask yourself: What are the same behaviors and actions that cause the same results and do not allow you to move forward?

- Think about successful people: What are the behaviors and actions they would take to get the results they want?

- Write down and focus on the new habits and actions that you want, and consciously think about them when you catch yourself doing the old ones.

- Change your 'I can't' or 'I should' to 'I must' and 'I will.'

DON'T DRIFT...DISCIPLINE

For any muscle on our body to grow, it needs to be exercised and maintained continuously. The same holds the true for everything we want to accomplish at work or in life. If you want to be accomplished in anything, you need to get disciplined in doing things that matter, that are important, to bring you closer to success and set you on the path to whatever you want to do in life.

Of course, there are times when we need to take a balanced approach, but discipline for me is really an intrinsic quality that we all should strive for. It comes from within and starts with you. Oftentimes, we are looking for all sorts of shortcuts – the new meditation technique that will set us free, the new set of motivational tools, and the new supplement to get our body fit. But these may (or may not) work for a week, a month or 3 months, and if it's not coming from within us, it won't last. We don't do hard things if we are not emotionally attached to them.

If you look at leaders you admire, or the most successful people, you will see the level of discipline they have in their lives, and in doing things that set them apart from others, things that others are not willing to commit to. It is an intrinsic self-discipline – a matter of 'personal will' as Jocko Willink, a retired navy SEAL officer, calls it. The difference between being good and being exceptional is how disciplined you are.

He continues by saying, "Those who are at work before everyone else are considered best operators." But that discipline cascades down to everything else they do. Willink rightly said, in his book Extreme Ownership, that discipline equals freedom. This is very true – once you are disciplined with the things that you know you should be doing, it sets you free to do other things that you claimed not having time for, but which were in fact just an excuse, with the blame pointed everywhere else but at yourself.

OWNERSHIP

One of the most important things I have learned, that really impacts how successful you will become, is to take full ownership of the results that you produce, the challenges, everything that impacts your results, or even your personal or social life. If I didn't own the results that were expected of me or my team to deliver, I would have never achieved the level and quality that I wanted. I always expect the highest results, but that can only be done if I completely own it. It is an attitude, and the fundamental block of any success. Blaming others or making excusing not only doesn't help but it actually hurts the team, the company, and ultimately you. In some cases, we don't want to even acknowledge the problem, or are afraid to accept that we made a mistake because we don't want to take ownership of the consequences. This will not serve the team or help it win.

Mistakes happen in the workplace, especially with complex problems, diverse teams, and tight deadlines. We should be able to acknowledge it, come up with better solutions for next time, or reach out to others for advice. We have much more respect for a person who takes full responsibility for their actions and results, don't we?

When we look at the great leaders and successful people around us, we wonder how they make the right decisions in stressful situations, or remain calm when faced with chaos and complexity. But what sets them apart in such situations is that they carefully choose how they respond. They don't jump to a conclusion and decide out of an emotional outbreak. This is a critical skill if you aspire to be a great leader and to be successful.

Often, what we do is react to situations without thinking, and we don't choose our behaviors but just act them out. We respond in the way our mind is wired and how we were conditioned. This may sometimes have catastrophic results in the workplace or in our personal lives.

Victor Frankl, the Austrian neurologist and psychiatrist, and a survivor of concentration camp, wrote a fascinating book "Man's Search for Meaning", in which he describes his horrific journey through Nazi concentration camps between 1942 and 1945, where he moved four times between different camps, including Auschwitz, while his family perished. Frankl said, "Between stimulus and response there is a space. In that space is our power to choose our response. In our response lies our growth and our freedom." This is a very profound thought that can guide us to make a shift in how we react and respond.

The best leaders and successful people train themselves and practice various scenarios for responding rather than reacting to the situation:

1. Think about consequences and bigger picture – What will you achieve by reacting in specific way (e.g. in anger)? Will the response and consequences be aligned with your goals or plans? How will the response best serve you, your family, or your project and company?

2. Realize whether you are responding or reacting – This is important, because it will give you clarity if you are reacting out of anger, a lack of control, sadness, jealousy or perfectionism. If you pause and think about the root cause of your answer or reaction, you will be able to respond in a wiser, more thoughtful way.

3. Don't react out of emotions – This relates to the point above, but you will also need to realize that your best response is based on facts.

4. Realize that you have a choice and different options – When you are faced with a situation where you want to rush to react and respond harshly, realize that you have a choice, and consider the consequences of your reaction. Count to three, if you must.

HABITS

"What we know from lab studies is that it's never too late to break a habit. Habits are malleable throughout your entire life. But we also know that the best way to change a habit is to understand its structure — that once you tell people about the cue and the reward and you force them to recognize what those factors are in a behavior, it becomes much, much easier to change."
– Charles Duhigg 'Power of Habit'

A study was done by Wendy Wood, a Provost Professor of Psychology and Business at University of Southern California, on a group of people that was given stale popcorn in the cinema in exchange for rating a move. Most of the people ate the stale popcorn despite the fact that they said after the movie that they didn't like it. It turned out that they ate it out of their habit of being in the cinema. But what this shows us is that we often do things without realizing it and a, "Thoughtful intentional mind is easily derailed, and people tend to fall back on habitual behaviors," said Wood.

From the time you get up in the morning until you go to bed – most of what you do in between is without thinking; it's automatic. I mention automatic because it is a very important feature of habits, because we don't even realize what we are doing and why we do it. In fact, 40% to 45% of our daily activities is habitual, according to Professor Wood.

Everything we do or want to do is a step towards accomplishing a goal or achieving something that we desire – that goal might be to get to work, to satisfy hunger, to relax, to feel wanted, to get a promotion, and so on. Professor Wood explains that, "We find patterns of behavior that allow us to reach our goals. We repeat what works, and when actions are repeated in a stable context, we form associations between cues and responses."

It turns out that our brain creates patterns of activities, thinking, and behaviors that we do constantly and become automatic, so it doesn't have to spend energy to think about it each time (a simple example would be how to walk or brush your teeth). Our brain developed habits, so it doesn't have to think about them repeatedly and can have the space to focus on doing what's more important, like new projects at work, creating new product, writing, studying, making decisions, and more.

When we behave out of habit, our mental activity and alertness drops in the middle of it. Research shows that once we develop a habit and do something on autopilot, our brain is almost inactive, and so is our decision capability related to that activity. For example, when you are driving to work, you don't think, "Ok, now I need to decide to indicate that I want to turn right," do you? You don't make these decisions any more. When you were driving to work for the first time, you perhaps needed to think about which street to turn right onto. Over time, it became automatic.

Habits are developed slowly, and it is very hard for us to change the habit without completely knowing what the cues of that habit are. We must learn how to identify which cues led to a particular behavior, called cue awareness, so that we are at least aware and know when the habit is actually happening. Oftentimes, with certain strong behaviors, we don't realize the cue and, hence, we do them automatically. For example, some people bite their nails without realizing it, and they may now understand what the cue is (i.e. why they are doing it).

Have you found yourself with any habit that you do without understanding why, and you only realize it once you've done it? The important part of a change is to do it slowly through first recognizing when we have the urge or need to do the habit.

All successful people understand the importance of small improvements, which underpin our progress and have a profound impact on the long-term improvement. Imagine if you made just one tiny improvement every day. That small change, done every day, will turn into a habit and it will become part of your subconscious.

In the Japanese culture, this is called kaizen, which literally means 'improvement' or 'change for better,' and is fundamental to their professional lives and personal relationships. But the Japanese also understand that to see the change, we need to commit to it. Very often, what happens is that we set a goal, such as something that we want to improve. We might get excited and motivated at first, but that commitment fades after a few weeks and we forget to keep up our commitment. This comes back to understanding the triggers and wanting to change.

The single most important thing is our full commitment and then acting upon it. Without it, we will return to your original state in days. We really must be disciplined. At the end of the day, the most successful athletes didn't achieve their gold medals without true discipline. Yes, we will have obstacles, bad days, and days where we just can't do it anymore, but remember, after winter comes spring and summer. Don't think your winter will last forever.

Start small. Don't overwhelm yourself with too many things that you think you should, or want to, improve. It will only confuse you and you won't be able to achieve anything. To change your behavior long-term, you will need to:

1. increase your performance little by little every day, and
2. change your environment to get rid of the distractions that may keep you close to your old habits and behavior.

> *"We are what we repeatedly do.*
> *Excellence, then, is not an act, but a habit."*
> *- Aristotle*

GROWTH AND FAILURE

There are no happy accidents that turn people into experts or that give people some special gift which allows them to live a happy and successful life.

We are not born into it. While some could be genetic, most of it is not. When we are born, our potential is unknown. We can accomplish whatever we can possibly imagine, and our abilities can be developed.

When we read about successful people or observe those around us who seem to have more success than us, be it better jobs, better relationships, or better health, what they all actually have in common is their constant hunger for growth and development. They never stop learning new things and upskilling themselves, their mind is always curious, and they want to push the boundaries of what is possible. All these characteristics underpin their growth mindset, which is critical to their progression.

> *"When you are in a fixed mindset, your success is a result of that belief. And all you will try to do throughout your life is to prove yourself against that fixed standard. In a growth mindset, challenges are exciting rather than threatening. So, rather than thinking, "Oh, I'm going to reveal my weaknesses," you say, "Wow, here is a chance to grow."*
>
> *- Dr. Carol Dweck*

Growth mindset is a scientific theory suggesting that with effort, persistence, and hard work, our intelligence and abilities can be developed. Dr. Carol Dweck, a psychology professor for Stanford University, showed through over twenty years of study of human development and psychology that our belief system about our abilities and potential fuel our behavior and predict our success. Dr. Dweck's early research was focused on how kids respond to failure, and shows how some children reacted positively to failures and setbacks, taking them as opportunities to develop, while others were completely devastated by them. Those kids who thrived on challenges adopted a growth mindset. They believed that with hard work, good strategies, and perseverance, they would eventually develop more skills and talents. Those who wanted to stay away from failure at all costs were in the fixed mindset.

> *"It's not how good you are. It's how good you want to be."*
> *- Paul Arden*

Very often, we see people who have very fixed beliefs about their abilities, what can be done or achieved, and what they can accomplish in their career or in life. For example, you hear at work, "This cannot be possibly done," or "It's beyond my capabilities." Perhaps we may see that in ourselves at times. We may think, "I'm not good at this," instead of "What am I missing?"; "This is too hard," instead of "This may take some time and effort,"; or "I'm obviously not good at finance," instead of "I'm not good at finance yet and keep studying."

People who don't progress through their lives or career only see obstacles that prevent them from achieving what they want, or what is achievable at all. They look at their abilities, skills, and performance, or even their health, fitness, and relationships as fixed and accept them as they are. This "fixed mindset," as Dr. Dweck describes, "makes us believe that our character, intelligence, and creative ability are static and cannot change or improve in any meaningful way."

You may see multiple examples of a fixed mindset around you. There might have been several projects or initiatives that were believed to not be achievable or were too hard to implement, and hence were abandoned. A project manager believed that the timeline was too short; there were no right skills or resources within the team; no right leadership or systems to support it; and the reasons why not could go on forever. Focusing on issues rather than solutions, and the things that would prevent the team from being successful would, indeed, bring no results.

With the right mindset and approach, even hard tasks can be achieved, issues can be resolved, and step by step, you will take the team closer to success. Remember that if an issue can be resolved with actionable tasks, you actually don't have an issue. This requires the right mindset to be in place, one that will see unlimited potential and the bending of the boundaries of what's possible.

This is what successful people do. If we look at the people whose success we admire, then we will see that they cultivate their growth mindset to enable their personal, professional, and social development and progression. Research shows that one of the reasons why we feel unhappy or frustrated in our jobs or personal lives is that we stop growing and progressing. We, as humans, are "designed" to evolve, and progress and growth is necessary to our wellbeing.

> *"If you imagine less, you will be what you undoubtedly deserve."*
> \- Debbie Millman

With the growth mindset, as Dr. Dweck explains, we treat any setback as an integral part of our development and path to success. I have felt bad, embarrassed, or fearful of my mistakes and setbacks, but I've learnt that they would only help me to grow. Often, I came out on the short end with my decisions, but every time I aimed to tweak my approach to do better next time.

Growth mindset keeps our mind sharp. In today's work environment, we need to keep up with new technological and organizational developments. Things are changing and won't slow down anytime soon. To be ahead, we need to constantly learn.

Sometimes we find ourselves in moments where our fixed mindset kicks in, but the important thing is to realize it, snap out of that, consider more appropriate approach and move forward. Through "deliberate practice" we can change it – we must be purposeful and systematic about what we want to change. What helps me shift when I find myself in a fixed state are the four simple steps outlined below. They require a focused attention, and once you go through them, you will realize how destroying and limiting your fixed mindset can be, and instead will focus on developing more of a growth one.

1. Be aware that you are exposed to limiting thoughts based on your past and learn to be aware of your fixed mindset thoughts. What I mean by that is that we are prone to reject new opportunities, not because we are not able to do it, but because we are afraid of the unknown. Our brain is wired to search past experiences and do only what is known and in our comfort zone. Remember that this is only your brain's response to the unknown. It wants to keep you safe and it doesn't like risks and any unpredictability.

2. Acknowledge that you have the choice. We all have a choice about how we react and respond to any situation. How you interpret challenges, setbacks, and criticism is your choice. Whether you apply a fixed or growth mindset, it will have a chain reaction in what will happen next.

3. Replace fixed mindset talk with a growth mindset voice. Personally, I have had many moments when I dealt with self-doubt and feared to take on new challenging projects, was simply procrastinating, or too

lazy to do something. We have all been there. Over the years, though, I have learned to replace those damaging thoughts of a fixed mindset with the empowering thoughts and beliefs for growth. When I doubted myself and thought, "Can I do this? This is certainly not for me. I don't have the talent to do this," I immediately replaced those thoughts with empowering thoughts, such as, "I am certain I can do this and I will learn along the way," "I have passion and perseverance to accomplish this."

4. Take action that focuses on growth. Without action, there is no progress. Without facing the challenges and new opportunities, you will never learn. You must wholeheartedly commit to the challenge and overcoming any setbacks that will come your way. Learn from it and adjust as necessary.

FAILURES ARE YOUR GIFT

It is no secret that our worst fear is a fear of failure. However, failure is actually a good thing. It is just an opportunity to begin again, learn from it, and to do it more wisely next time. Encouraging our fears and failures prompts the most necessary changes in our lives and businesses. This may be true, but we don't often feel or think like that.

When we make mistakes, we feel terrible and disappointed; we lose confidence, and get discouraged. We just don't want to continue or go through it again. What we are actually doing is missing out on the primary benefit of failure. Winston Churchill once said, "Success is the ability to go from one failure to another without losing your enthusiasm." The man was right.

When it comes to failures, our egos are our own worst enemies. When something is going wrong, we try to save face and our defence mechanisms kick in, and we often find ourselves in denial. It seems very hard for us to admit and to try to learn from failure, because it requires us to challenge our status quo.

> *"I haven't failed. I have just found 10,000 ways that won't work."*
> - Thomas Edison

Look at Walt Disney, who was fired from the local newspaper he worked for because he was told he had no imagination. What his story teaches us is that just because you encounter a setback or end up on another path, it doesn't mean that you are stuck. Keep learning from your mistakes, apply changes to make things better, and you will get back on track eventually, and most likely, you will be better off than before.

There are many successful people who we can mention here who have failed but never gave up, e.g. Steve Jobs, Oprah, JK Rowling. What separates successful people from those who are unsuccessful is that they have a huge amount of perseverance. They never give up or let their failures define them. They pick themselves up even stronger than before and keep going. It's not always easy to continue moving forward, but when you keep pushing onwards, despite the failures and obstacles along the way, you are already ahead of all those people that just gave up. I find that the secret really is to just show up and try your best over and over again.

Failures are part of the process. To be successful, you must learn how to make it a tool rather than a roadblock. You must be adaptable and agile. When you stop learning from your mistakes, then you will stop growing and developing. You should take any failure as motivation in pursuit of your dreams. Don't let it stop you but grow you instead. The only failure there can be is when you quit. Learn the lessons, apply them, and you will come out stronger than before. You will never learn faster than you will by executing something.

NOTHING HAPPENS WITHOUT ACTION

Remember, talk is cheap! Action is everything. Our thoughts are catalysts to get started. But our thoughts are not things, and nothing will happen without taking those thoughts and putting them into action mode. That's what successful people focus on. They know that talking, planning, and analysing won't get them too far. It's their actions that will trigger all the things on their road to success. To be successful in any part of your life, you must be action-oriented. Mark Twain said, "The secret to getting ahead is getting started." You can't do everything at once, but you can take it step by step. Incremental changes every day will work in the long run.

Try to keep the momentum to get you closer to where you want to be. You can develop a plan to work on your habits and then pick one to focus on at the time. Commit to it!

BANNISTER EFFECT

One of my favourite stories, which I would like to finish off with and which I personally find very inspiring, is the story called The Bannister Effect. In moments of doubt or thinking that something is not possible, I always return to it and remind myself that what I might believe is not possible can actually be achieved. Before 1954, it was believed that running one mile under 4 minutes was physically impossible, that the human body could not possibly do it. In 1954, Roger Bannister, an English middle-distance athlete, ran it in 3.59 minutes, breaking what was believed to be an impossible record. But what happened next is remarkable – once it was known that the mile could be run in under 4 minutes, many other athletes accomplished it, and with even better results.

What this shows us is that it was not a sudden leap in the evolution of the human body that broke the physical barriers. It was a shift in thinking. Bannister truly believed that it was possible to run faster and break the record. He visualised himself achieving it over and over, and his mind accepted it as reality. The story also shows us that once we see that something can be done, something that was once believed to be outside of our realm of possibilities, we can also achieve it.

In our daily work or life, our mindset has the ability to limit us or set us up to achieve the impossible, not only for us but those around us, our team, our peers, and our family. We are in control of whether we will conform to what is socially accepted or try to believe beyond it. If Bannister believed that the record was 4 minutes, and nothing could be done about it, that it was a physical limitation, then he would never have been able to break it. He would never even have tried to do it.

Just like this story, what often keeps us from achieving what we truly want is the barriers that only exist in our mind.

To connect with Anna Griffin please visit www.ReimagineThePossible.com

Break Down the Box

Taking a Risk to Create an Amazing Life

KIRK JAKESTA

B ecome who you were meant to be.

Listen to that voice in the back of your head that says, "I could do this."

Growing up as a young man, I quickly adapted to the lifestyle that was presented to me, a life that threatened to consume me, sending me into the dark path of life, if I were to let it. Where the thought of change seemed out of reach.

Perhaps you grew up in a lifestyle like mine where drug and alcohol abuse were the norm, where selling drugs as a young adolescent wasn't unusual but accepted, or you grew up in a good wholesome environment where life just made you comfortable with what you had. Deep down, we always want more. We want the best that life has to offer. In the back of our mind, our thoughts tell us that we are not worthy of it. We deal with the hand life dealt us and face the tough financial challenges without a leg to stand on, believing that we are not worthy of better.

Just getting by was my specialty, and still is. It was my normal growing up. My father who is now in his mid late 70's, worked his ass off for a better part of 60 years of his life in order to provide. Working construction camp jobs, spending half a year and sometimes more away from home to be able to provide a comfortable living for my family and I. Now, even though there isn't anything to retire on comfortably he has finally come to terms with retirement due to his health limitations that come with his age.

My mother, who is one of my best friends, is in her late 50's now and she suffers from Osteoporosis and for me that's a hard pill to swallow. Seeing your parents' health deteriorate, especially after growing up thinking that we will all live forever. My parents have been the best, they gave me a good life. Despite growing up the way I did, my parents have been my crutch, and shaped me into the man I am today. Teaching me what's right from wrong, teaching me to be a gentleman, a provider, a man that can achieve great things. Along with the influence of my brothers and grandparents and other family members throughout my life, I want to be someone great, for them.

We all have close friends and family, whose aging has brought the reality of losing them closer to mind. Many of us have lost close family and friends to sudden loss. As life goes on, it's clear that we are all living off of borrowed time, tomorrow is never promised, and the best time to create a life worth living is NOW. My loved ones inspired me, and I want to inspire those who need it. To show that no matter where you are in life, there is always a fork in the road. If you are brave enough to look past the fear of starting something new, then you will realize that life's greatest experiences are usually on the other side of fear. I want you to recognize that you deserve to tap into the greatness inside you! There is more to life that we are missing out on.

Previous years have brought some amazing opportunities my way, but first, I had to let go of my fixed mindset and adapt a growth mindset. I had to take action and show up to reap the benefits. I'll admit, it took a major shift in my thinking, and it's a constant battle against procrastination, self-doubt and fear of failure. Even as I write this chapter, I realize that it took a lot to get to this point. I had to crawl out of that hole of self-pity, dust myself off and get back into the game. I needed to step beyond what I saw as possible in my everyday life, and instead believe that I had what it takes to propel me forward, only if I was willing to take that leap of faith to create significant change.

Starting with my first self-development program, a seed was planted in me. I gained the mindset to be my own boss one day. To stop working 8-12 hours a day on another man's dream. When we think about how much free time we have, how much of it is wasted? Think about it; the average person sleeps 8 hours a day and works for 8 hours a day. That's 16 hours dedicated to sustaining a living and getting the proper sleep. There are 8 remaining hours that most of us aren't taking full advantage of. I know there are other essential activities that are accounted for in those 8 remaining hours, but you get the gist of it. I came to recognize that I could make my life extraordinary, but I NEEDED TO CHANGE MY MINDSET to tap into my ability. One of the hardest people you will ever have to battle is yourself.

Imagine stepping out on faith like that in your life. Having a vision for your future and then taking a leap without the proverbial safety net. My leap led me to many mentors and opportunities. Opportunities like becoming an award-winning author by taking the leap and jumping into a book deal with an amazing powerhouse, world renowned speakers, authors, entrepreneurs, and now my co-authors, with the goal to pursue a speaking career to inspire First Nations people around the world and starting my own digital marketing agency to serve small to medium sized businesses and help them survive during a pandemic. Note that all those opportunities gave back to me in a big way. They helped me to mentally prepare for the next opportunity, the next open door, and the next chapter in my journey towards an amazing life.

Each step I took led me to another networking opportunity, another inspiration, another mentor, and the momentum continues to build. I put myself on the path to find those "once in a lifetime" opportunities. Now I want to reach out to my people, becoming a role model and demonstrating that all things are possible. There is a life outside of your conditions, which is the reverse of the way you are living. It is possible to create a brighter future, but it starts with believing in yourself. Dedicate yourself to something, then great things will happen. You do not have to be a victim of your circumstances. Instead, you can take charge and be the change in your life.

You do not have to remain affected by our grandparents and parents unfortunate past of residential school, and the horrible ripple effect of what they went through. For those who don't understand what they went through, that ripple effect has affected us all through the generations in one way or the other. Now is the time to stop that ripple effect by making conscious choices in our lives to create change.

We must take responsibility for our past choices and actions, but more importantly, the ones we are making in the present. The present is all you can change, but the possibilities are endless if you are willing to move through the fear of the unknown and the fear of failure.

The point I want to make throughout this chapter is that you have the power to create, to build, and to change. It all starts with a willingness to open your mind to the possibilities and even to take risks to achieve what you have always dreamed of, even if you may have denied your ability to create that vision in the past.

I am here to tell you that all things are possible. You do not have to struggle through an endless loop of paychecks, overwhelming debt, and the hardship of not having the necessities. You do not have to let a troubled past get in the way of your amazing future. Instead, you can have a life that is rich in personal meaning and leaves a legacy behind for your children and grandchildren.

CULTURE IS THE FOUNDATION FOR GROWTH

Our culture is one based on close-knit families and time-honored traditions. For hundreds of years, we lived in harmony with the land and each other. Time has changed things, and modern life does not seem to focus on this rich cultural heritage. I even find that the way I was raised limited my access to my culture, disconnecting me from what should be a greater part of my life, although I believe strongly that it is never too late to learn and make it a part of my family's life. I will continue to put forth the effort to make that happen even if it's with only little snippets throughout our lives.

What cultural heritage am I referring to? I am First Nations. I represent Nisga'a Nation, from the village of Gitlaxt'aamiks or New Aiyansh, and from my father's side. I am part of the Tahltan Nation. These are parts of who I am, although I truly wish the connection with these cultures was an even stronger part of my daily life. Still, it doesn't stop me from being who I am.

Why isn't it a greater part of my life? My childhood was not easy. I would say that I was undereducated, as the school system in my village was rated the second lowest in British Columbia. On top of that, we had a house built in the early 2000's. A few years after we moved in, we had a kitchen fire. It did a lot of smoke damage to the kitchen, leaving it completely charred. Nothing was done to fix it. That is a mindset that I grew up with, one where you learned to live with what you had. There wasn't an expectation that we deserved to have the kitchen fixed and, 15 years after the fire, that damage is still there. This is the reality of where I came from and who I am. So, you can see why I would want more out of life.

What about your own life? Can you see places where damage was done, but you did nothing to fix it? All of us deal with some type of psychological, physical, or emotional trauma. It could be a result of choices we made, or the actions of others that were not in our control. This world is a cruel place. In the end, however, it is up to you to decide if you want to live as a victim or be a victor instead.

Growing up with my two older brothers, I was confronted with circumstances that I could have blamed for my life choices. At home, there was a lot of fighting, drinking, and smoking weed. It was a tough environment for a young adolescent but that was my normal. Around 15 or 16 years old, I went from being a recreational marijuana smoker to dealing the herb. In fact, I became one of the biggest weed dealers in the community at one point. Then I moved to hustling harder drugs, to the point where I was making good money for a teenager. I didn't feel that great about myself or what I was doing to get that money. However, the lifestyle was so different from the years that my family struggled that it was hard to turn my back on the money.

That all changed the day that one of my friends offered herself to me as payment for drugs. It felt like an incredibly low point in my life. I started asking myself what I was doing. This was not who I was meant to be. I was completely shocked by her offer, and I couldn't accept it. I ended up giving her the drugs for nothing and quitting that business. I was done contributing to tearing down myself and others. Now I had to figure out how I was going to build myself back up and, in the process, how I could help others do the same. The answers were still a few years away, but I was at least on the track to finding them.

If I had not stopped then, I could have ended up in jail, dead, or with the death of someone else on my conscience. Your choices create your future. By making the choice to get out of that life, I changed my own future and I am grateful for it. I learned at a young age that life is truly about moments. Moments where you can either take the road less travelled or the same one as everyone else. Even though I didn't acknowledge it back then, I was making these life-changing decisions. I can see now that my conscience was in the right place.

That rough environment offered few opportunities for young people like me. As I got out of the drug world, I realized that I couldn't stay where I was. I needed to create an opportunity for myself. So, I headed to Vancouver, where I attended Vancouver Island University Trade School. I took classes to be an automotive service technician. After graduating, it became clear that this wasn't the future for me either. The men in the trade hated their jobs, and I realized I didn't want to be one of them. I was at peace with that. Even though I dedicated almost a year of my life to achieve that certification, I knew deep down I couldn't sacrifice my life to unfulfillment and regret.

I felt as if I was going through the process of elimination. The knowledge about what didn't work for me was as valuable as the knowledge about what did work for me. I started to understand myself better and believe that my happiness was mine to create.

CREATING HAPPINESS STARTS WITH YOU

Happiness is not going to magically appear because of the things you own or the fact that you work 60 to 80 hours a week to bring home a paycheck. Instead, happiness is a state of mind, one that you can create, no matter your circumstances.

My determination to create change in my life led me to leave behind a life of drug dealing, and countless dead-end jobs. For almost a decade, I have lived in Vancouver, where I started to do all kinds of different work, exploring my interests and trying to find my place in this world. I learned a lot about what I was good at, what I was okay at, and what I just struggled to accomplish.

During this time of exploration, I was still a typical young man, out to meet girls, party and live life for the weekends. Not the most ideal lifestyle, but it was the life of a young man with few responsibilities. Then my daughter was born. She is my biggest inspiration, and I knew that I wanted to give her a better life than the one I had. Now I was inspired to do better, even if I wasn't sure how. I believed that if I did almost everything in the opposite way I was raised, I was going to be fine. In order to do that, I needed a new set of skills, and I needed a new way of thinking about the world and my place in it.

It was about becoming the role model that I wish I had when I was growing up, and finding inspiration in the young girl that now depended on me. To give her happiness, I had to be willing to claim it for myself to be able to provide a better life for her and my entire family. I'm a strong believer in "When I make it, we all make it."

Your happiness is a state of mind. You are in charge of your mind, not your circumstances. You can choose what to dwell on, and your point of view. I want to challenge you to recognize that you need to change your mindset about the circumstances themselves, thus creating happiness for yourself no matter where life currently has planted you.

IS NEGATIVE THINKING HOLDING YOU BACK?

Some individuals seem to naturally be able to find the silver lining of any situation, and their joy in life is apparent. Even when they are faced with difficult circumstances, they focus on what they can learn and how they can grow, instead of becoming defeated. Granted, that does not come naturally to everyone. In fact, many of us are quick to fall into a negative way of thinking, one that keeps us focused on what has gone wrong and keeps us from acting decisively.

The reason I point this out is because if you want to achieve real change in your life, you need to be able to act decisively. A negative mindset will keep you from acting, simply because you will spend all your time talking yourself out of doing anything. The excuses can be numerous. Here are just a few:

- I don't have the money.
- I don't have the education.
- I don't have the skills.
- Those adventures are for other people. I have a family to take care of.
- The risk is just too great.

Negative thinking means that you tend to value the risk higher than the reward, so you freeze yourself in place, living with circumstances that you aren't excited about, simply because you can't accept the potential of risk.

Now if you aren't able to accept risk and you have a negative frame of mind, it can be very difficult to create the happiness you seek in your own life. It must start with a change to your own mindset, one that acknowledges risks but is not defined or held down by them. At the same time, I am not talking about a pie-in-the-sky type of thinking, the kind that cannot recognize challenges or potential issues.

Risk assessment is still a part of life, but the focus needs to be on how to mitigate the risk, not how to avoid acting so that you can avoid the risk altogether. When your mindset is in a positive frame, you are going to find that you look at risk differently. It is not an impasse or an obstacle that stops you from moving forward. Instead, you view it as something to be addressed, a challenge that can be navigated effectively. For every problem in life, there is a solution. The only thing that stops us is fear itself.

When you are focused on just surviving, and not on thriving, then no matter what soil you are planted in or the circumstances that you find yourself in, you are never going to be truly happy. In the quest for small moments of happiness, you are likely to make choices that are going to negatively impact yourself and those that you love.

Those choices could be anything, from bad investments, addictions, toxic relationships. The point is that, long term, those choices are going to negatively impact your ability to make your situation better. Instead, you have now made your road even harder. Now you have another set of challenges to deal with, and those additional difficulties can be truly crushing to your mind and spirit.

Can you relate to some of these choices or ways of thinking? Can you understand negative thinking and using words like "can't," "won't," or "shouldn't" are keeping you from achieving what you were put on this earth to accomplish? As you can see, negative thinking can break down your spirit and leave you feeling as if you don't have the strength or ability to create change in your life. It can leave you feeling that your life is what it is, and you are better off just to accept it. I'm here to say f#!k that. Go Get Yours!

You are never truly stuck unless you choose to be. Can you find some light in the darkness, that inspiration and motivation you need to take the first step? I found it in my daughter, but it was also clear that I was changing my thinking and that was impacting my future in ways that I couldn't yet imagine.

MANIFESTING YOUR NEW REALITY STARTS WITH YOU

During the time before my daughter was born, I had that moment all new fathers do, questioning the finances and trying to figure out how to provide for this new miracle in my life.

My answer was civil construction, which led me to eventually becoming a heavy equipment operator. I picked up the experience needed by jumping into a piece of equipment every chance I got. Straight up, I manifested that into reality. I had it in my mind when I first stepped foot in the field as a laborer, watching the guys run those big machines, that one day "that would be me."

Are there areas in your life where you need to be aggressive to achieve a goal? I could have sat back and waited for someone to give me an opportunity to learn how to operate those machines, but the truth is, that day might never have come. By seizing the reins, I created the opportunities for myself and achieved my goal. It wasn't easy, and I had to make some sacrifices. For two years, I worked the night shift. Starting out as the lowest paid laborer (which was still good money for a new soon-to-be father) and working myself up to be a lead hand. Delegating tasks and executing them in a safe timely matter. Here is where my life revolved around eating, sleeping, and going to work. I couldn't do anything else, and it wasn't the healthiest lifestyle. But it was also the first time that I manifested one of my goals, and it wasn't going to be my last.

In spite of all that negative thinking from my past, I decided to take a leap beyond what I had already accomplished. I decided that I didn't have to work to barely make ends meet for the rest of my life. I did have the ability to leave something for my daughter, and I had the power to create a legacy, one that would impact the generations to follow. The question was how?

START WITH INSPIRATION AND ADD ACTION

No matter who you are and where you are in your life, there are individuals who inspire you. They are the ones who accomplish so much, despite the challenges and those who tell them that it can't be done. Yes, there are plenty of people out there who are going to tell you that nothing can change, you are risking too much, and that you will be sorry later. They might even claim that they are telling you these things for your own good, so that they can protect you.

That is not the kind of protection that you need. Instead, you need to be willing to take the risk, even be willing to fail. Fail forward. After all, if you never fail, then you will never know what it takes to succeed. You need to step beyond the opinions of others, beyond the fear, to have more, be more, and experience more.

To put it simply, failure is just a way of eliminating a process that wasn't going to work, thus allowing you to focus your time and energy on other options that might be more successful. At this point it is not a secret anymore.

It's out in the open and has been for decades; failure is the crucial ingredient for success. You must treat each failure as part of the elimination process, one more step closer to achieving your goal. Eventually, something will give, and you will get the right idea or find the solution to your problem. This is a guaranteed result of dedicating your thoughts to your goal, and you best believe it works to the opposite effect as well. Your thoughts navigate your life. Whichever road you choose to go down is directly controlled by your own thoughts.

My goal was to achieve a better life for my family, and that meant figuring out what I was good at and what I wasn't good at. Simply choosing to abandon a course of action that isn't working can feel so liberating. Plus, every time you remove yourself from a course of action that isn't working, you are moving yourself closer to achieving your goals!

The inspiration for my next course change came as I realized that my mind was not fully in my work. I operate heavy machinery, which is not a job where you can afford to be distracted.

Instead, you need to stay focused on what you are doing and keeping the people around you safe as you complete the task at hand. Once I realized that I was in the place where I couldn't keep that level of focus, I knew I needed to take a break. It was my moment to take a leap and see where it would lead. I was inspired by several individuals, ones who took risks and were willing to give everything to make big changes in their lives.

Even though at the time, after a bit of a hiatus, the skills that I picked up after all those years have given me the credibility to take on a supervisor roll after only two months coming back to the same line of work. That is a testament to the dedication that I once had to this specific line of work. Even though I knew this wouldn't be for the rest of my life, it feels good to know that I have what it takes to walk on to a new job, take control, and quickly establish myself in a key role.

What are you willing to give up? I bet you might be thinking that you aren't willing to give up much. Your life is comfortable, you have a routine, and even if it isn't everything that you hoped it would be, at least you understand the rules and expectations. That is where we all get tripped up from time to time. We choose the devil we know versus the devil we don't, because the unknown is scary. It is a dark hole and we don't know what might be hiding in there or lurking just around the corner. The truth is that what is lurking around the corner could be amazing, but too many times, we miss those opportunities because we are afraid to look.

Part of changing your mindset means accepting that taking leaps is critical to your success. The unknown is a place that allows you to grow and really craft your vision for your life. Fear is what keeps us in one place, holding onto things that might not benefit us, but are comforting because of their familiarity.

Think about it this way. If you know how to achieve a result using one process, you are likely to continue to use that process. However, if that process doesn't work as well as you like, you might explore other options and open yourself up to the idea of trying something different.

While that might work in the processes you complete at work, when it comes to taking greater risks in your professional and personal lives, there is a tendency to do the opposite. We tend to focus on dealing with the broken process, instead of trying to find an alternative and exploring other opportunities.

On the other hand, when I opened my mind up to the possibilities, I also unlocked my potential to create the life I had envisioned for myself. Therefore, be willing to be open to the possibilities. Do not lock yourself into one way of thinking, thus creating tunnel vision regarding what you are capable of accomplishing.

Even if the way that you are doing things has been successful in the past, you need to remember that life is not black and white. There is more than one way to skin a deer. What works successfully for one individual might not work as well for you. Don't be quick to lock yourself into one way of doing things, and thus be unwilling to consider other options.

Our world and society are geared to locking you into a position or a way of thinking, and then discourage you from taking the chance to make a change. Yet, those who have been the most successful, the ones who have created real shifts in how our world functions, started out by taking risks, breaking out of the expectations that had been put on them.

It is adapting a growth mindset and never accepting defeat that helped me to start a business in Digital Marketing as well as becoming a published author and one day a speaker that will inspire countless Indigenous people around the world. You can create that type of change in your life too! You just have to be willing to stop worrying about what people will think of you. Succeed or not, it's your life. Do what's best for YOU.

It involves breaking out of the box, taking a risk, and then reaping the rewards from stepping onto the path less traveled.

UNDERSTANDING THE EXPECTATIONS THAT KEEP YOU LOCKED IN

A part of any society is the fact that expectations are built into how we are shaped. Cultures include specific events to mark our passage into adulthood.

From our courtships through the building of our families, certain expectations are put into place for all of us, based on where we grow up and how we are raised. What can happen, however, is that those expectations can end up being roadblocks that keep us from moving forward and tapping our full potential.

In my childhood, there were multiple roadblocks; circumstances that could have kept me stuck on a path that left me feeling unfulfilled and unable to care for my daughter in a way that I wanted to. I could have continued the cycle of drug dealing and dysfunction, but I decided to go out into the unknown. You have the power to do the same!

Therefore, I want you to think about the expectations that are part of your life. Are they serving you now or are they blocking you from moving forward? The biggest problem for some of my people is that the expectations are often set too low and our resources are often limited, and we are left with the acceptance that we have reached our full potential.

However, I know that there is more out there for all of us. It starts with a willingness to act on our own behalf, not waiting for someone else to do it for us. We must lose that sense of entitlement because nobody owes us anything. It's up to us to put forth the work that is needed to achieve what we want in life.

Every belief and value you have contributes to the decisions you make, and how you choose to act. Those beliefs and values can be altered as you experience different events throughout your life. Now you can choose to take those experiences and allow them to help you sift through those values and beliefs.

Do you regularly take the time to examine your values and beliefs? Do you ever ask yourself why you believe what you do, or why you value one thing over another? The reason it is important to do so is because you are going to make automatic decisions that impact your future based on those beliefs and values. Shouldn't they reflect who you are now instead of who you used to be?

Recognize that, whether you want to or not, you are constantly being exposed to influences that are changing and shaping you. How are you responding to this shaping? Many of us don't even consciously recognize how we are being altered by these forces, but once you are conscious of how these influences are impacting you, you can choose to accept or reject them. Take this for an example: McDonalds has their advertising everywhere. Literally globally. Everywhere you look, whether it's a billboard, on social media or television. Advertising for their new promotional meal or drink is constantly being programmed into your brain, so when you are hungry or thirsty you subconsciously have the thought of the new stuff instantly pop up in your head. This is all brainwash. The same goes for anything you allow into your brain, even a daily dose of inspiration. So be cautious of what you allow in and choose wisely.

Part of the importance of recognizing these influences is that many of them can keep you in a state of denial about the possibilities in your life. Others could be trying to keep you safe, so they discourage you from taking what they believe to be unnecessary chances. Still others are just negative in general and will tend to bring up everything that could go wrong, every potential obstacle, and even attack your intelligence for thinking about giving it a try.

Notice that those influencers in your circle are fundamentally trying to block you from taking a path that they may have decided not to walk themselves. They truly believe that if a course of action wasn't a fit for them, then it is not a fit for you. It is often the way that our communities, including family and close friends, try to keep us in their circle, but it also leaves many of us trapped in a life that does not benefit us, or allow us to fulfill our potential.

I am here to tell you that it is possible to create a life that you are excited about, one where you can take risks that bring you greater rewards. My life is altered, and I am excited about the future because I opened my mind to the possibilities beyond operating heavy machinery. Now, I am an example to my daughter about pursuing her dreams, regardless of where they take her.

As you shift your mindset, choosing to buck the beliefs of others, you are going to find that you repel those that continue to have a negative frame of mind and start to attract those with a positive and open mindset.

Throughout my journey, I have made decisions based on what inspires and motivates me, not on a fear that I need to get back to work. I am not counting the days until I need to report back to work or let them know that I am not coming back. Instead, I am enjoying this adventure. I am excited to see where it leads me because I know, even though I am not there yet, I am closer than when I first started.

You cannot let fears, especially those of a financial kind, keep you from taking leaps. So many of the inspirational individuals in our world took leaps without a financial safety net. They didn't have an emergency fund or a set date when they would no longer pursue a goal if they weren't successful. They believed in acting to achieve their goals, no matter what financial challenges came their way. An unshakable desire to success. They adapted WIT in their lives, which stands for "WHATEVER IT TAKES."

I want you to take on a mentality that allows you to focus on achieving your goals and overcoming the challenges involved. When you give everything to your efforts, you will see them come to fruition. It starts with recognizing that the people you surround yourself with are going to push you to try harder and go further, or they will focus on trying to pull you down and break your spirit.

CREATE THE CIRCLE THAT SUPPORTS AND INSPIRES

The reason that I want to talk with you about the people you spend time with is that they are going to be part of those forces that influence you for good or bad. If you have specific goals that you want to achieve in life, then you need to surround yourself with those that will support you working to achieve those goals, while at the same time holding you accountable when you are working contrary to what you want to accomplish.

In the years since I moved to the mainland, I met someone who proved to be my biggest supporter and best friend, my dear love Amanda. As my significant other, she has the most influence in my world. If she had tried to stop me from pursuing my dreams, it might have meant the end of my journey. Instead, Amanda chose to step out in faith with me.

Without her, I do not believe I could have accomplished so much, so quickly. She stood by my side, took the leap with me, and our lives continue to blossom. She inspires me to never give up. I have found that surrounding myself with people who push me to be better and take chances are going to give me the fuel necessary to keep going, despite the challenges.

If you spend time with individuals that are not supportive, eventually you will give up. Your goals and dreams will remain unfulfilled and, years later, you will find yourself with regrets over what you should have done, instead of a sense of joy and accomplishment for what you have done. Remember, it is all about the influences that you allow in your life. Studies have shown that we become like the people that we spend the most time with. Who do you spend time with, and whose thoughts and ideas are you being exposed to on a regular basis? Do you have someone that you just know is in your corner that you are confident is adding value to your life?

It is easy to quit when you feel like you have no one in your corner. Amanda and I have been through many tough times, but the point is that we continue to stand together. You need to build that same type of support system, but also be willing to be that support system for others.

I want you to start focusing on how the people around you talk and act. Are they taking risks and inspiring others to follow their dreams? If not, you could be surrounding yourself with naysayers, those who are more likely to try to tear you down than build you up. If you want to make a change in your life, you need to first change your mindset, and then change who you spend your time with. After all, if you are changing your mindset, you need to spend time with individuals who will help you to reinforce that change.

Part of the way that I help myself to stay focused on a new open mindset is by choosing mentors that inspire me and give me critical food for thought. They help me to set my mind up for success. It is not about abandoning who I am, but recognizing that there is more to learn, to do, and more ways to grow as an individual who contributes to my culture and traditions. I also realized that they helped to set up my mindset to take even greater leaps and enjoy the opportunities that are available. It is not about the money, but about the fulfillment that comes from inspiring and being a role model for others from my community.

I choose to surround myself with mentors and associates that respect where I have come from, but who also challenge me to go further and to explore what the world has to offer. I want to leave a legacy for my family, but also to my people. I want them to recognize what is possible for ourselves and our nations. If you believe in yourself, you can achieve a lot in a short period of time, with or without a college education.

If you feel as if the darkness of life is overtaking you, I want you to stop and take an inventory of who you are surrounded by, and what type of encouragement they provide. You might find that they are taking light away and making the darkness appear that much worse.

The world is growing and changing constantly. We all have the wisdom born from our experiences, knowledge, and skills. Part of what makes us rich as human beings is the passing of that wisdom to others. When you find a mentor, you are finding a source of wisdom that you can tap into for your own benefit, and the benefit of those around you.

Start by looking for those that inspire you and then finding ways to interact with them. It could be through their writings or even their speeches. Use that inspiration to help motivate you to act. When you work with a mentor, you will find that you are pulled into their circle, and that will allow you to grow your circle with like-minded individuals who will help you to make the necessary changes to achieve your dreams.

I made some dramatic changes this past year, but much of that work started earlier. When I opened my mind to alternatives beyond the world I was living in, I started to believe I could act and create real change in my life. I saw the possibilities, and it was an exciting time. Still, I admit to having some fear and trepidation about whether I should actually move forward and take this leap into the unknown.

This is where your circle is so important. They will provide encouragement during those times of doubt, and when you wonder if you are truly capable of doing everything that you have ever imagined. Amanda provides that encouragement for me, and I like to think that I am just as supportive of her dreams. It is not a one-way street, but one built on mutual support.

Doubt is the enemy of those who want to build a different life, who see their purpose on a path that is not traditionally followed by those around them. You have the capacity to fight against that doubt by fueling yourself with positive thinking and gathering the tools you need to act.

What are some of those tools?

THE TOOLS THAT CAN INSPIRE YOU TO CREATE

I have already spoken about how important it is to create a circle that supports, encourages, and holds you accountable to create real change. This includes finding mentors and inspiring figures. You do not have to feel limited to just one mentor at a time. Mentors can be part of all aspects of your life, both personal and professional.

Depending on what you want to achieve, you may look for a specific type of mentor who has already walked that path. Over time, you may find yourself choosing another mentor because you have achieved your first goal and are now focused on another aspect of what you want to achieve, which requires help from another individual with experience and skills in that area.

My mentors were chosen because what they said inspired me, motivated me, and gave me food for thought. Remember, my world experience was fairly limited before I started down this path of life. Yet, once I got started, it helped me to reassess my life and understand that nothing was truly out of reach. I just had to act.

Another important tool is to find a means to keep yourself centered on your goals and objectives. The world has a way of naturally distracting us from our goals and objectives, simply because we are presented with challenging circumstances that can appear out of our control. Therefore, it is important to find ways to allow your mind to quiet, thus giving you the opportunity to refocus.

There are a variety of ways to do this. I know some individuals find that peace and clarity when they take the time to exercise daily. Others prefer meditation, taking the time out of the morning and evening to clear their minds through breathing exercises or other forms of meditation. Still others prefer time in nature, where they can reconnect with the air, soil, and animals that are part of our home.

Whatever your preferred method, I want you to make it a regular part of your routine. You can focus on the vision of your achievements, giving them life and very clear details. The point is to make them as rich as possible to make them as real as possible. When you focus on visualizing yourself successful in achieving your goals and endeavors, you will empower yourself to create. You can see yourself acting in a way to reach those goals, which serves as the inspiration to keep you moving forward.

Athletes use visualization techniques all the time to achieve their goals. Doing so, those athletes are inspired to keep up the thoughts and actions that will allow them to do what they want and achieve their goals. They have created a mindset that gives them the ability to be successful, no matter what challenges might come their way.

I find that visualization helps me to manifest my dreams and goals into my reality. The richer the detail, the sharper the image, the faster I can make it happen. Discussing these ideas and dreams with my partner also helps me to see it clearly in my mind. Ask yourself questions to help you flesh out all the details.

Our ancestors often gathered for ceremonies that allowed them to make decisions which guided their course. It was early visualization, and I want you to tap into that. No matter where we are from or how we were raised, we all have the power to create inside of us. Our connection with each other and the earth is what allows us to find success, regardless of the challenges that come our way.

We all have encountered mental quicksand in our lives. It comes in many forms, but we need to be vigilant in looking out for it and avoiding it wherever possible. If you find that you have fallen into a quicksand trap, then you need to stop for a moment, allowing yourself time to reset your mindset back on the path you want to take.

Those resets are not easy, but they can be done with mindful and conscious effort. Do not be quick to assume that just because you were distracted or pulled into that mental quicksand that you cannot pull yourself up and move forward. The fact of the matter is that you will have moments where you fall, where you feel doubt, and where you wonder if you really can be successful. I want you to recognize that when those moments come, you need to walk through them.

It will not always be easy, but it is necessary that you make a conscious effort to do so. It will help you to grow stronger and also give you the endurance necessary to achieve anything you want in life.

When I took my leave of absence, I truly did not know what was going to happen next. However, I left myself open to whatever possibilities presented themselves. Essentially, you have to train yourself not to immediately say no, but be willing to say yes, no matter how crazy or ill-prepared you might feel for the situation. I had to open my mind to the possibilities and be open to exploring what the world had to offer, without fear.

I believe that what you want to achieve in life, you have the power to attract. The universe will give to you what you focus on. If you focus on the positive aspects of a situation and the possibilities available to you, you will draw more opportunities to yourself. A path you might never have embarked on will open up right in front of you. It is this power that you need to tap to create a real directional shift in where your life is headed.

One of the effects of creating change for yourself is that you end up being able to impact others. After all, you do not live in a vacuum. While others are influencing you, you are influencing others.

Think of how great speakers can get you to think differently, can inspire you to act differently, and can chart a different course for various institutions. I want you to recognize that you have the same power within you. We all do!

I want you to be inspired to see the valuable person that you are and use that vision to create and build a future that can be a guidepost to others. There are so many ways to impact others. Like a ripple in a pond, those efforts can spread farther than you ever imagined! Here are just a few of the ones that can give others a jolt of inspiration and leave you with joy and love in your heart.

Volunteer – Do you know how many organizations need volunteers to achieve their missions? You could work with young people, old people, people who have been dealt horrible circumstances, those struggling to overcome an addiction to drugs or alcohol, and so much more. You have the power to influence their lives for the better, just by your presence and a willingness to listen. Always remember that whatever inspires you, there is likely an organization trying to move that agenda forward. Take part and recognize the gift you give when you give of yourself!

Invest – I am not just talking about finding the right financial investments. I mean invest in people. Be kind, be willing to forgive, and be willing to lend a hand. When we invest in each other, then we can create large-scale change. Jesus Christ is credited with saying there is more happiness in giving than in receiving. Give to others and see how it benefits your mindset and inspires you to keep those investments going.

Mentor – I also want you to recognize that you can serve as a mentor to others. It is a gift that keeps on giving, one that can allow you to pass down your wisdom to others. Mentoring is not a top-down affair. Someone that you mentor can also inspire you as well. Be open to the possibilities and you can truly be a gift to another individual looking to create change in their life.

As you can see, my life is in motion right now. I am writing, investing, and creating the life that I want, one that will allow me to care for my family and pursue those items on my bucket list. I chose to move away from a dark path based on the past choices of myself and others to create one that is filled with light and laughter. You don't have to be chained down to a way of living that leaves with a lifetime of regrets. Instead, I want you to focus on what is possible and then make it a reality.

There is no vision that is too great or too small for you to achieve. The biggest obstacle that you will ever have in your life is the one that you create by means of your mindset. When you choose a positive mindset, you are blasting that obstacle out of the water. Do not see risk as something to avoid, but rather as a means to achieve even more in your life.

I want to inspire you and help you to move forward in creating dramatic change in your life. I am always available via social media, and for those who know me, feel free to see how we can work together, how I can serve as a mentor, or even just share with you what inspires me to get out of bed and keep my focus.

I hope that you recognize that the darkness in your life does not have to win. You can let in the light and achieve more than you might have dreamed was possible. For those that need a boost, see my story as one that you can create for yourself. Recognize that I am just getting started. Your willingness to pick up this book means that you are ready to take a leap, and are just looking for the motivation. I hope I have provided that! May the life you want be manifested in your reality, and may you tap into your creative abilities.

"Use Your Struggles Today As Motivation For Tomorrow"

— Kirk Jakesta

Please visit Kirk Jakesta's website for more information, www.StreamLineToSuccess.com

Five Key Elements for Success

Shift to the Next Level

ALANA LEONE

There are moments in our lives when we have an opportunity to change our path, to explore in a new direction, and to step out into the unknown. Too often, doubts and fears can take hold in our lives, limiting the risks we take and the amount of success we can claim.

I want you to change all that. I don't offer this lightly. With the power of opening your mind to peak performance thinking, you are putting yourself on the path to generate the success you want in your life.

Now, to be clear, all of us have different definitions of success. You are already successful now in some areas of your life. Now let's take that to the next level.

It involves laser focusing on what you want instead of being stuck with what you don't want. By creating a drive to pursue your desires and ditching your limiting decisions and beliefs, your life will take on a whole new meaning. You leave the plateau and reach new heights. You feel energized! It takes stepping outside of your comfort zone and overcoming challenges instead of creating obstacles. It takes climbing one step at a time to the next peak.

As part of my work, I assist people to make the transition away from their fixed thinking and their inability to take advantage of the possibilities around them. Instead, I invite them to open their minds and explore what success they can claim through a shift to next level thinking. I give them the strategies, tools, and behaviors to be able to do it themselves.

Part of a mindset shift involves removing the sting of failure. I often tell my grandson, "What a lie of the mind it is to think you are going to start something brand new and you are not going to fail."

It is what you do with the failure that gets you to the next peak or leaves you stuck on the plateau. Take what you learn, implement it, and then do it again. When you take failure as feedback, it becomes less personal. If it is something you have decided you want, you will do it. Look at when you first learned to drive. Did you fail? If you are like me, then you likely did fail every day until the day you didn't. I didn't quit. You likely didn't either. I took what I learned and got back behind the wheel. This process is a strategy for success. It's a tool you already used in other areas of your life — only, you forgot.

Your mind likes to put you down and keep you safe. Mine too! Now I say thank you to my mind and make a shift to the next level. I have control over my mind, not the other way around. Too often, we attach negative emotions to failure. Instead, recognize it as a positive learning experience, one that is meant to assist your growth. There is potential in all of us to change, to alter ourselves and our circumstances. Too often, we allow our circumstances to turn into a much bigger obstacle, one that quickly becomes a blockade in achieving our goals and desires.

How can you push through the blockade? First, determine whether you are thinking with a fixed mindset or an open, curious one. As you explore your thinking patterns, you will be able to blast through the obstacles and blockades your mind has created.

As part of this journey, I am going to share with you the importance of five key elements for success. You can achieve success with these elements just by taking one step, then another — to shift to the next level.

PUSH THROUGH TO SUCCESS

When you operate with a fixed mindset, there are a few elements that come into play. One of the first is how you talk to yourself. In a fixed mindset, your self-talk tends to have a negative aspect to it. Time and again, you tell yourself that was a stupid decision. , You ask yourself "Why did you think you could do that?" or "Don't take the risk!" There is a lot of "No, no" and "Wait, wait" throughout that list.

Plus, when your self-talk is full of negativity, and on a constant repeat, then you quickly begin to believe what you are telling yourself. A vicious cycle starts, one that cannot stop unless you make a conscious effort to do so.

That self-talk also impacts your reality. After all, if you think you are not capable, then your subconscious mind is going to seek out the evidence of that from your surroundings. It reinforces that negativity.

Your subconscious mind is listening to the words you say. It believes that these words are what you want. That is why I cannot say it enough: Think and say what you want, not what you don't want. I catch myself doing this all the time. I frequently ask myself, "Is that what I want? If not, then change it right now!" Once you spend time focused on the positive or what you want, then you will see it leak out of your mind through your mouth. Then it moves from your mouth to your actions. It is a beautiful sight and sound. Once you experience it over and over, you feel amazing.

When you push through a negative mindset, you make the conscious choice to focus your thoughts around a positive viewpoint. There are many tools for your toolbox in the world today, and you have to be willing to use them. You gain the discipline to keep on top of it. Look at football or any sport you love. The coach is there every game and every practice to push through negative mindsets and motivate the team. The coach doesn't come at the first part of the year to give the team a pep talk and then nothing the rest of the year! He constantly pushes and reminds the team, "You got this!"

How can you make these new decisions? The first part of any new strategy is recognizing what decisions to eliminate. Recognize that eliminating one negative decision or belief means another positive decision of belief must replace it. Otherwise, within the vacuum, your old ways are likely to return.

Next level thinking is about pushing yourself to identify those unproductive patterns within your subconscious way of thinking and shifting them into what you desire. Often the best way to address limiting decisions and beliefs is through a conscious dig into your past.

Past experiences and decisions create limiting decisions and beliefs. In turn, that past creates a root cause, likely within the years of your life up to age seven. In fact, without learning from the past issues, you are susceptible to another limiting decision or belief based on the same root cause. Think of a tree with lots of fruit on it. You automatically assume that the roots of the tree are flourishing. However, there may be rot that is not visible to the naked eye. The same is true of your life. There may be root causes that keep you from flourishing but are not easily spotted.

Let's start with examining what root causes are and how to tear out those rotting roots and replace them with nourished, healthy roots for your life and your business.

ELEMENT #1 - ROOT CAUSES

First, let's start with how you are thinking now and the impact it has on your life.

We all have a story that starts with detailed events and ends pointing the finger at someone else, declaring them guilty of some misdeed. In many ways, this is the story of self. What you believe about yourself and others in your story gets ingrained further through a spiral of negative thoughts and actions.

The more we talk about this, the deeper it gets driven. At some point, the body starts to feel the emotions in other ways, such as sickness, depression, rage, and anxiety. A trip to the doctor for a pharmaceutical cure focuses on the ailing body, but not the root cause in the spirit.

As you think back to the main events of your story, I would like you to come up with an age when an event occurred. Are you two, four, six, ten or twelve? Now I would like you to think about how long you have been preparing and restructuring this story of the past into your conceptualized self. This part creates an identity. There is usually a lot of emotional baggage, often sadness, anger, fear, hurt, and guilt. You end up feeling trapped and making decisions based on those emotions. Thus, you create a pattern of self-sabotage or procrastination. You want the procrastination to go away, but it goes much deeper than just procrastination. The cause is deep in the soil and the roots, corroding and rotting them further.

It becomes a deadweight in your life, one that keeps you from pushing forward. How long do you want to be trapped by those emotions, the hurts, and the negative energy that comes from these stories in your life? How long is enough for you to hurt before you are done with it? When do you decide that it is time for you to have the freedom to push forward?

Our childhoods are not dictated by us, but by the people who surround us. Parents, extended family, and others impact who we are and the experiences that we have. Those experiences shape our beliefs about ourselves and who we are in the world. However, there are also those of us who grow up in situations based on past hurts. Those older adults do not know how to address their past hurts, so they pass those hurts onto their children. It becomes a generational hurt, one that has roots so deep it can be hard even to address them.

They have all done the best they can with their experiences. This reality may be hard to hear, and it doesn't give people a pass for being this way. However, they were that way, and now it is up to you to push forward and make different choices because you can see a different path. The best thing you could do to get back at them is to have massive success and joy.

Let the events in your past propel you to impact your present and future for good. You might want to break that cycle of negativity and rot. However, that can be difficult because you don't know any other way to think, feel, or behave. What do you do?

Our society is changing, and the next generations are determined not to carry that heavy emotional and mental baggage into the future. Their choice to address these issues or root causes means developing new tools. My passion is to share these tools with others for the next generations and our nations, thus transforming our world with information and education.

One aspect of shifting our thinking is in recognizing new teachings about how to harness the power of your mind. Some people were taught about the mind, how powerful it is, and how it helps to keep us safe. Some people were taught that we have control over the actions of our mind. We are not powerless over our thoughts. You are programmed with certain beliefs and values. The good news is, if you want to change the old programming, then you can.

Shifting your negative beliefs and useless values can take courage. In the end, however, it is a very cleansing experience. By that I mean, when you settle past hurts, you can address your emotional baggage and set it down for good. How can you set that past baggage down?

Part of that is based around the principle of forgiveness. When you forgive someone, you free yourself from any power they might have over you, mentally and emotionally. Forgiveness involves letting go of any resentment and refusing to allow them to hold you emotionally hostage. Often, while you might be hurting, they might not even still be thinking of you or even remember the hurt that they caused. That person might even justify it in their minds, believing that it was for your good.

In the end, you have the power to decide how long you are willing to let the actions of others impact you. It is up to you now to take responsibility in your choice to stay stuck or push forward. It is not always easy to make that decision and stick with it. Emotions can come into play, essentially sabotaging your efforts. When you choose a path and stick with it, then you find that shift in your thinking. The most effective way is to remove the emotion around the event and come up with some learnings. This process is what I have mastered. Do not let your mind come up with excuses. Rid yourself of the past burdens and fly free.

My passion is to give people tools to clear those emotions. It is important to remove the toxic negative emotion — the root cause — by filling your roots with a powerful positive emotion. You need to give yourself the tools to drain the emotion of a memory. Doing so will allow you to be at peace with those events and then push forward with your life.

Another important point is that you can have positive root causes as well. Those are the memories and emotional ties that helped you understand your purpose or gave you a belief system that continues to support you.

Positive roots can also be a way to connect with others. When you have a positive experience, it tends to color your day and make you more inclined to try and do the same for others. Shifting your thinking involves taking those positive root experiences and allowing them to help you gain a deeper understanding of yourself and to deal with others in a kind, generous, and loving way.

I love the metaphor of the tree. Roots are so critical to the life of the tree. Without proper care, then the tree will eventually die from a lack of food, water, and stability. Think of all the ways that your roots provide stability in your life. They ground you, give you a sense of the world you live in, and social rules that help you to operate in that world. Negative root causes can be damaging to your internal root system, thus threatening your stability and the means by which you can continue to grow and flourish in your life. Granted, it is possible to save the tree, but that means you need to do the hard work to address the rot. Addressing rot involves self-care and hard work, as well as creating new patterns that will nourish healthy roots.

Essentially, addressing rot can save the tree. Plus, when you take the time to care for your roots, both positive and negative, then you will find that your tree is healthier and more stable.

When you see a tree with toxic roots — the leaves are brown and sparse — there is evidence of compromised stability. It is dying a slow painful death. After some time, the tree will fall over in a windstorm. Move to a picture of a tall, healthy tree with strong roots. This tree will have a lot of leaves and be strong and confident in its stature. It will also have big, juicy, and excellent tasting fruit, and live a long, healthy life.

The healthier the roots, the more productive the tree and the more excellent the fruit. Your life can be the one you have always imagined, but only if you are willing to change how you interact with the world by addressing the various root causes within your background. I want you to be a healthy tree, not one with sparse and brown leaves, struggling to survive the windstorms of life.

Now you need to look at your roots. Are they healthy or can you detect some signs of rot? When you detect that rot, it is important to address it right away. Next level thinking means not allowing thoughts, emotions, and events to fester and cause further damage. At the same time, when you address those root causes, then you are dealing with the damage already done.

I want you to understand that it is possible to get your roots healthy and keep you growing and thriving. Next level thinking focuses on helping you understand yourself better, including why you react a certain way, and why certain situations trigger specific emotions. There are always root causes.

Addressing them will help clear the way to change how you react not only in these situations but in other stressful circumstances and wind storms.

I am passionate about helping individuals detect the rot in their roots and then ferret it out. Once you clear the damaged roots, the tree (you) can flourish and grow toward your goals and dreams without that dead weight. Part of that process is not only clearing the negative, but also helping new roots grow in place of those old roots.

Too often, people focus on those old root causes and make them the obstacle that keeps them from pushing forward and embracing new ways of thinking. However, when you decide that you will address those root causes and that they will no longer be obstacles, then you can begin to see the new possibilities that await you! You begin to look for new roots.

Recap:
- Root causes impact our beliefs and values, how we think, and our self-talk.
- Addressing root causes can leave room for new growth.
- Work with me to clear out your rot and clear the obstacles in your path.

ELEMENT #2 - NEW ROOTS

To be even more successful, you need to recognize the responsibility you have in your life to choose change. You are in charge and have the power to shift your beliefs and values. Your experiences give you valuable learnings, so you can reach out to expand and flourish. Your mindset controls your behavior. When you take the knowledge and leave behind the emotional sabotage, you will train your brain to search and keep busy looking for positive information.

It is like a puppy that is full of energy. When you aren't giving the puppy something productive to do, then it will eat your shoes. Keep your mind busy with actionable thoughts and productivity, thus training it to work for you and find even more creative ways to keep busy. Your mind will spiral up and not down. Give your mind something powerful to focus on.

Shifting your thinking can help you transition into the type of thinking that will allow you to envision a new path for yourself and then work to achieve that change. To have more success in all areas of your life, you need to recognize that you and only you have the responsibility of choice — and to change your environment. You are the one that has to move your foot forward to take that step.

I can help you decide where you want to place your foot, but you need to be the one to take that step. As you create new roots for yourself, it will be easier to push forward. Recognize that you are teaching yourself a new skill, one that is going to require you to step outside of your comfort zone. Like any new skill, it might feel awkward at first, but over time that awkwardness will fade.

I want you to stop for a moment and think about the language you use when trying to do something new. There are phrases that you can use which will indicate how successful you can be. When you start with a negative mindset and speak negatively about what you are attempting, then you are likely to find yourself giving up if it is not successful on the first try.

Too often, people focus on what they are doing wrong or they ask "why questions." For example, "Why does this happen to me?" Notice when you shift your mindset and start to create new strategies and processes, you begin to look at what you are doing that is amazing. Then you might start asking yourself, "How do I focus on expanding that positive energy?" Positive thoughts and energy attract more positive thoughts and energy.

Now, shift that language to more positive language. Do you see the difference in how willing you are to keep going in the face of challenges? How you talk about something and what you focus on about that item or experience can help determine if you will be successful or not. When you say, "I can get into this," it is positive. When you say, "I won't be able to get this done," it is negative. Pay attention to what you say. It is very important. The point of new roots is that you are changing your focus and how you speak about the events in your life.

I want to push you to step outside of your comfort zone and think about how you talk to yourself and how you talk out loud to others. What are you truly ordering up on the menu of life? If you are not clear and using clear, positive language, you are probably going to continue to find your goals thwarted or the delivery being less than what you had hoped to achieve. You think you are ordering a 12-course meal, yet you get back liver stew.

After taking my four years of training, I realized that I now had a skill that would help me push forward in my life and to create an amazing future for myself. I know how to talk to my goal-getter, and the results have been incredible. I want you to have the same experience. By taking the time to look at your mental language, you can find the patterns or places where communication is breaking down and create new positive processes.

It is up to you to create new roots and allow yourself to be at peace with your past, just as it was up to me to do that for myself. Once you put all the pieces into place, then the possibilities are endless.

When you are defining your new roots, you need to have a laser focus on what you want. Distraction can keep you from achieving what you want. If you find that you are distracted, remember that you do not have to stay that way!

Part of my pushy training is about pushing you to move past those distractions and to regain your focus. You have control over your thoughts. Consider your thoughts as leaves on a running river. If you are standing on the bank of the river, then you will see those leaves floating passed you. Your thoughts are also moving at the speed of a river, so you need to decide which leaf to grab.

That is how you need to focus, simply by picking one positive thought or idea and then giving it your full attention. When you focus on a pattern of negative thoughts, then you are going to find that type of energy coming your way. However, when you immediately decide to focus on the positive, then you draw that positive energy towards yourself.

Here are just a few examples of the types of positive energy that you can create with your thoughts: love, understanding, and compassion. It is about flexibility to focus and also to dream and live in a creative space.

Now that you have an understanding of how you can control your thoughts, you can identify the patterns that could be obstacles in your life. The obstacles are a tapestry of limiting decisions, negative beliefs and values, to name a few. These drive you to take action or not. If your drive in the past has allowed you to coast, then we need to push the gas pedal. Change involves making the move to throw the bags out of the trunk, thus lightening your load. Then press the accelerator to the mat and take off!

Recap:
- Shift your thinking from the negative to the positive.
- Take control of your thoughts. You have the power!

- Create a laser focus on what you desire to achieve.

Now, I want to shift your focus to the last three elements I will be discussing in this chapter.

ELEMENT #3 - PURSUE YOUR DESIRES

Align your life and business to your desires. We have looked in detail at the root causes and received the learnings and released the negative emotions from the events. We have created new roots and realizations. You are thinking about things differently and in a new light. Now you may have determined what you want and may even have a vague idea of how you are going to get there.

You may find that, now, you are ready to focus on how you are going to achieve the life you desire or even to focus on the fact that such a life is possible. Remember, use direct and clear language with yourself and others that defines a specific path. If you don't do this you might not get what you expect, even though you followed the path. Your words and phrases need to be in alignment with the possibilities. The various parts of you need to be integrated, and then you need to decide on a clear path.

As you sharpen your definition of the life you desire, you give your mind something to work with. Start by asking great questions of yourself and others. Get curious about what you like and what you don't. When you work at home, which tasks tend to go quickly, and which ones tend to drag on and on?

Define your strengths and weaknesses. They can help you see what areas might be creating challenges in your life that you need to address. How can your strengths work more effectively for you? What might you need to go learn more about to turn your weaknesses into strengths?

One of the best ways to truly define the life that you desire is to visualize yourself in the life you want today as if you already have it. Write out in a journal that ideal and desired life. Give it as many details as possible. Include what it feels like, sounds like, smells like, and looks like. See yourself there and then describe that image. Act as if it is today you have what you want. I am sure that you might have done something similar in the past, but now that you have looked at root causes, it is time to do it again. What you focus on only gets bigger as you get accustomed to taking those massive actions! Focus on the desire.

One caution about focusing on your desire is to not stay in the future all the time. It is a beautiful dance to be able to be in the present most of the time and also focused on the future at times. It is about putting the desire in the future with you in the picture and then being in the present to complete the tasks.

It is also about fun. Being in the present is fun. I will straight out start belly laughing in the middle of something, and people say, "It is her laughing time." That laughing time is catchy though, and others soon start to laugh along. It is also my process for bringing me back into the present. I enjoy floating around in the future, sometimes too often. The action happens in the present.

You want to have everything you ever dreamed of in your life. You and I only get one chance at this life. What is holding you back? What are you going to do about it? Clearly, throughout our discussion, I have identified some root causes that you need to consider, as they could be blocks. However, I have also shared a few points to help you address them. Now I want to connect with you to help you to shift your thinking and keep going on the journey at my website, www.pushycoach.com.

Recap:
- Define your desires.

- Determine what is holding you back.
- Don't stay in the future, but keep a foot in the present.

ELEMENT #4 - ACTION

All that I have talked about throughout this chapter has led to this element, the one regarding action. Too many of us focus on the fear of a situation, and that keeps us from acting. However, when you focus on what you want — I mean laser focus — that fear will go away. You will move forward, despite the fear.

You must choose your mindset. Success is a decision. Not having success is a decision as well. A positive mindset takes work. It's like working a muscle. The more you go to the gym, the bigger the muscle. The more you focus on your positive mindset, the better the chance of getting that desire. You make the desire bigger and brighter, bigger and brighter.

When you learn the pattern of clear focus, then your vision gets bigger, clearer, and brighter. Focusing on the future and then acting on that vision means you are focusing on the future and not on the past. It is a sure sign that you are growing strong roots and are ready to move forward.

When you do make strides forward and an obstacle gets in your way, or you fail at something, it could be easy to decide to quit. A lot of people quit and tell themselves, "I guess it wasn't meant to be."

Keep your power and the ability that you have to be successful. If you are starting to do something that you have never done before, why would you expect not to have obstacles or that you might not have failures along the path to success? It is unrealistic to think that way.

Put positive processes in your mind every day. Give your mind exercise. Going back to the coach story, you recognize that coaches are consistently telling you new teachings and giving you more motivation — not once, consistently! Doing small things consistently is the key.

People get busy doing tasks that have nothing to do with their desire and then the day disappears — a week, a month, a year, ten years. Act now.

Additionally, it is critical to have a support team in place to help you as you transition to your shifted life. This is why I love setting up Mastermind groups. Masterminds are where like-minded people get together to work on a clear direction and get the wisdom and experience from the entire room, not just yours alone. Who is in your support team? Think about the people you rely on for advice, encouragement, and motivation. Are they providing that or are they bringing out the negative and showcasing a critical spirit?

Recognize that to build a positive support team, you need to be willing to be a positive support to others. That quality will draw people of like-mind to you. Do not be afraid to let go of the people that are limiting you, despite your efforts to be supportive of their dreams. Perhaps letting go of that relationship will make room for greater opportunities, including the chance to meet new people who can join your inner circle.

My point is that I know you are going to achieve great things. Do you know it? Once you do achieve them, it is important to celebrate and express gratitude to help keep those positive roots nourished.

Recap:
- Take the first step to create success.
- Build a support team.
- Be supportive of others, and it will return to you!

ELEMENT #5 - CELEBRATION AND GRATITUDE

Probably the best part of achieving anything in life is the satisfaction of knowing that you accomplished what you set out to create. That can be the push you need to start a new project or create a new chapter in another area of your life. I always believe in celebrating your successes, as it can be a true source of motivation and inspiration. However, celebrations do not have to be limited to times when you accomplish something or are successful in an effort. Find at least one thing to celebrate everyday!

When I do my talks, I ask the group if they have celebrated themselves that day? I always raise my hand. My hand is often the only hand raised.

Why is this the case? You are so good at being hard on yourself that you are not good at celebrating yourself and your accomplishments. Without your struggles and obstacles, then you would not be who you are. You are an amazing individual, especially because of your blemishes and scars. Your marks say who you are, and they make you the strong person you are. That is something to celebrate.

The point is that celebrating yourself is meant to push you forward to the next level and shift your thinking to bring you the life you desire. Part of that process involves being grateful for what you have achieved already. Gratitude is something that you can pass on to others, and it creates a positive energy that only grows.

Part of celebrating yourself involves exploring what you enjoy and trying new things. When you find fun things to do, then they keep you in a great state of mind. You have the choice to create your day your way, so why not start as soon as your eyes open! Starting this way could be the most comfortable and rewarding process of your day.

Recap:
- Celebrate what you have accomplished.
- Be grateful for your abilities.
- Explore new things and step outside of your comfort zone.

SHIFTING YOUR THOUGHTS STARTS NOW!

Here is a 10-minute process for you to begin shifting your thinking first thing in the morning. Do it consistently. Before even setting your feet on the ground.

This process is known as the "Push through to your purpose" process. It is given to you from the The Pushy Coach®. I created this so that people can shift their thinking even before they put their feet on the ground first thing in the morning. When does the mind start with its noise? Right — first thing! Beat your mind and put in the shift of positive energy before your feet hit the floor. You can do this process even before you are out of bed or while you are still stirring. I call this process the easiest process because you are still in bed. You can begin to build healthy roots for your amazing life from the comfort and warmth of your own bed.

1. Decide and choose this time to not only wake up physically and emotionally, choose to wake up consciously and to live on purpose.

2. Set an intention for your day. Intentions are critical for taking action. Some examples to get you started.

    a. I am open to new positive experiences today.

    b. I experience myself of service to others today.

c. I am 100 percent present and aware with others today.

   d. I experience myself healthy, wealthy, and unconditionally happy today.

3. Say three to seven gratitude statements. What are you happy about? Some examples to get you started.

   a. I am grateful for the sun.

   b. I am grateful for my family and/or friends.

   c. I am grateful to have woken up this morning.

   d. I am grateful for the fresh air today.

4. Celebrate one success from the day before.

5. Say, "I like myself. This day is the best day ever!"

6. Visualize great things happening today. Get up you amazing person.

7. Repeat the process daily.

The secret is to focus on what you want. With these few new things to do, even before you get out of bed, you will be creating a great add-on to the success elements that you are already making a part of your life.

To do something different — to break through your comfort zone barrier — is part of living your desired life. When you get proactive to your outcomes and desires and less reactive to limiting decisions, beliefs, unaligned values, and more, then you can truly move your life onto the path that allows you to have an amazing life journey.

You can say you didn't know before, but now you do know. To live and to pursue your desired life is a choice you can make or not. Taking action is a responsibility. Consider yourself pushed. If you need a bigger push, then contact me at www.pushycoach.com or ask us about our 1-year "Shift to the Next Level" coaching package and also how to get the bonus 5-hour "Breakthrough Experience".

I believe in tearing out the old roots so much that I want to get you a fresh beginning by taking the "Breakthrough Experience" before starting your Next Level Coaching to get you to the next level in your life. In the Breakthrough Experience, you can learn to release root causes, and in the "Shift to the Next Level" coaching, you can lock in new roots to pursue your desired life with action. Take action and celebrate yourself and others with gratitude.

I appreciate you, and I thank you for taking the time to read through and learn about next level thinking. With you here, it also helps me move forward to a new way of thinking. When you think about it, there is always a next level, and we can do it together.

To learn more about Alana Leone, please go to www.pushycoach.com

Developing Resiliency in the Face of Adversity

TIM DELOSO

"Character cannot be developed in ease and quiet. Only through experience of trial and suffering can the soul be strengthened, ambition inspired, and success achieved."

– Helen Keller

It may be trite, but the only constant thing in life is change. Life will inevitably throw a curveball (or more) at you. No matter how hard you try to control your life, you will undoubtedly come face to face with a situation that will throw you off your game and leave you lying face in the mud, wondering how such a thing ever happened!

In such situations, you have three alternatives: (1) Do nothing; (2) Think about doing something; and (3) Actually do something. I'm sure most, if not all, of us would not choose the first alternative. After all, who wants to stay in the mud??? In the second alternative, you start thinking about getting up, but the slippery ground makes it hard to stand up so you decide to just wallow. In the third alternative you take action and try to get up. Despite slipping back down and after making several attempts, you eventually regain your footing and head home ready for a shower.

What distinguishes those who do nothing from those who actually take action? It can be summed up in one word: RESILIENCE. It means getting up to begin, and begin again, without giving up. Even during the most trying times of your personal or professional life, you must meet challenges with a resilient spirit in order to achieve your dreams.

In over 30 years of climbing the corporate ladder with large, multinational companies, I discovered that some of the most challenging and uncomfortable situations were responsible for uncovering new paths to advancement and happiness. Large multinational companies are notorious for constant change and setting high standards for their employees.

Restructurings, mergers, stretched goals, corporate politics and trade wars rock these companies' professional environments and demand resilience from corporate warriors. Intelligence, hard work, discipline and focus certainly help with one's career, but these qualities are not enough to survive in challenging times. That is where resilience comes in.

CULTIVATING RESILIENCE IN UNCERTAIN TIMES

"I learned that courage was not the absence of fear, but the triumph over it. The brave man is not he who does not feel afraid, but he who conquers that fear."

– Nelson Mandela

In this chapter, I want to share with you why it is critical to cultivate resilience. And not just resilience, but HABITUAL RESILIENCE. It is not enough to just survive or tolerate one or two of life's curveballs. Anyone who does so is at risk of becoming skeptical, negative or downtrodden. Instead, one must develop the habitual resilience needed to meet all curveballs head-on and turn every crisis into an opportunity.

Speaking of crisis.... as I write this, the global economy is being ravaged by the COVID-19 pandemic. We are witnessing an unfortunate and devastating loss of lives and means of livelihood. In the United States alone, tens of millions of workers were unemployed at one point as a result of the changing economy. My heart goes out to all those people. The virus has adversely impacted the travel, hospitality, entertainment, retail and restaurant industries, not to mention churches, schools, offices, sporting events, gyms, governments and public services. Even after lockdowns are lifted, many experts believe our laws, attitudes and day-to-day activities will continue to be different from the way they were before COVID-19. Life as we knew it has dramatically changed!

Many feel like the rug was pulled out from under their feet by not being able to attend church services, watch a ball game or visit an exotic destination to name just a few. Humans are social beings who thrive when they can nurture friendships, celebrate memorable events, bond in sporting events and explore new horizons in person.

We are left with many burning questions:

- "How can we continue to grow as individuals and as a community when we can't congregate?"
- "How can working parents cope with the responsibilities of childcare while juggling Zoom calls?"
- "How can people worship their God in public?"

Despite all this, I am a big believer that "when a door is shut, many windows are opened." Resilience can be your superpower in these challenging times. The more you strengthen your own resilience, the more you will be able to not only survive, but even thrive. Witness how people are connecting with long lost friends, seeking business opportunities and raising money for charitable causes—all online. Others are actually enjoying working from home close to their families, with no commute and working in their sweats!

Let's investigate what resilience is and how important it is for your life. Even if you identify as a resilient person, I urge you to read on, as you may discover new tools for even further development. We will talk about the need for a positive attitude. We will examine the importance of being an explorer. We will see how resilience is built up by going the extra mile and never giving up. Lastly, we will talk about the importance of taking action. Are you ready? Let's dive in!

DEVELOP A POSITIVE ATTITUDE!

"Success is not final, failure is not fatal: it is the courage to continue that counts."
– Winston S. Churchill

When you are working toward your goals and transforming your life, you will face challenges, make mistakes and suffer setbacks. Remember those curveballs? However, if you focus on what you can control, you will discover one thing that can make all the difference: your reaction.

I know this is easier said than done. No doubt! Some psychologists say it takes 30 days to develop a good habit or overcome a bad one! So start small, by changing your reaction to little things that challenge you throughout the day. For example, do you let irresponsible drivers get to you? Or are you able to rise above it by wondering if they had a family emergency and wishing them well? Do you let cloudy morning skies during summer prompt a reaction that the day "will be dreary?" Or can you rejoice in cooler weather instead of blistering heat? By rethinking your reactions to these common triggers, you will habitually block undesirable events from derailing your positivity.

A positive attitude can also be enhanced by a sense of gratitude. Gratitude encourages you to recognize all the good that exists in your life right now and reminds you of all your past blessings. That recognition can help you remain positive in the face of challenges and setbacks.

I also like the idea of keeping a journal filled with uplifting quotes. If you haven't noticed, each section of this chapter begins with an inspirational quote. Why invent your own words of inspiration when so many great people such as Helen Keller, Nelson Mandela and Winston Churchill to name a few, have already supplied history with such memorable ones? Fill your journal with records of your accomplishments, positive feedback or acts of kindness. These affirmations can be from clients, co-workers, family members and friends. Jot down whatever makes you feel good and helps you remember your goodness! Why not include images that produce happiness? Happy images help keep your spirits lifted especially during days when more than one curveball has been thrown at you.

Consider seeking professional advice. Not every challenge can be overcome by yourself. Oftentimes, you need a mentor or coach to provide independent and different opinions on how to overcome setbacks and achieve success. I have had coaches for my spiritual life, family life, professional career, investments, personal fitness and change management. I have also coached and mentored numerous professionals who felt stuck in their careers and couldn't advance to the next level. If you want to achieve your goals and get results faster, coaching is an indispensable tool.

Stay positive! You want to set your mind up in a particular way where you can see change and negative events in your life as flexible, short term situations you can easily move on from. Attitude is an indispensable part of achieving resiliency. As you cultivate an attitude of positivity, you will gradually see resilience develop in your body, mind, heart and soul.

BE AN EXPLORER!

"Two roads diverged in a wood and I – I took the one less traveled by, and that has made all the difference."

– Robert Frost

Robert Frost ignited a passion for adventure in many a soul with his famous passage as read above. However, in 30+ years of corporate life, I have met many people who felt trapped in their jobs and who did not have the courage to explore other opportunities. Even now, the pandemic has caused people to be even more fearful of losing their jobs, which may cause them to be even more hesitant than ever to explore other opportunities. However, it is precisely in these times that one must be an explorer! In his best-selling book "Who Moved My Cheese," Dr. Spencer Johnson illustrated how following the same path can lead to failure. Some mice continue to look for cheese in the same spot of the maze where it used to be and are unable to find it, while other mice are more adventurous and ultimately find it by being explorers.

When you find yourself at the fork in the road, do you seize the day and take a calculated risk, or do you stay on the same road with the same predictable outcomes? By taking calculated risks, your spirit for exploring and taking the path less traveled can create the most rewarding experiences! Some say the two saddest words in the English language are "If only." Regret is a horrible feeling to live with, so be more open to new paths.

GO THE EXTRA MILE!

"Start by doing what's necessary; then do what's possible; and suddenly, you are doing the impossible."

– St. Francis of Assisi

A friend of mine once gave great advice to my teenage sons that I would love to share with you. He said success comes to those who do 10% more than what was required. Let that sink in… just 10% of extra effort can differentiate you from other people and spell the difference between success and failure!

Were there office meetings where you could have been more prepared and contributed greater insights? Could you have spent another 5 minutes with your child asking how their day went before putting them to bed at night? How about kissing your spouse goodbye rather than mumbling "Sorry, I'm late for work," and rushing off? As they say, "Pay now, or pay later." Regret for missed opportunities can be difficult to bear in the long term. That extra 10% is powerful and makes developing resilience feel more possible!

NEVER GIVE UP!

> *"Never give up, for that is just the place and time that the tide will turn."*
> – Harriet Beecher Stowe

Perseverance and resilience build on each other. The more you persevere, the more resilient you will become, and the more resilient you become, the more you will persevere in challenging situations. When you persevere while being resilient, you will come across opportunities others ignored.

For example, in challenging economic times, many people will be tempted to quit their jobs and start a business. Unfortunately, the failure rate of new businesses is very high. According to the U.S. Bureau of Labor Statistics, about 20% of new businesses fail within their first year and 50% by the end of their fifth year! Beware of "get rich quick" schemes that promise an easier life but often don't work. History is full of famous startup successes such as Facebook and Airbnb, but these are the exception rather than the rule. Instead, pursue business opportunities that require less time, effort and cash outlays while offering higher chances of success.

One of these paths could be as simple as sticking it out with your employer and earning a stable income with health benefits. Climbing the ladder in your current organization is often a far safer method for achieving your financial goals, especially if you are the sole breadwinner of a family. It also helps develop the perseverance and resilience needed to not take the easy way out by quitting your job. If you do have an interest in entrepreneurial opportunities, try to get promoted early on in your career to provide enough savings to confidently experiment with them. This two-pronged approach means checking out career websites such as Glassdoor and LinkedIn AND reading Entrepreneur magazine; soliciting advice from successful executives AND networking with business owners; or working a full week AND emailing potential clients with a service to be provided only on Saturdays.

If a side hustle is too much for you, passive investments are a good way to supplement your income. For example, instead of renting, look for bargain-priced homes and become a homeowner.

The bottom line is this: Wherever you find yourself on your journey right now, I urge you to not give up and walk away. Keep pressing forward and remember that you build resilience one step at a time through perseverance. The rewards for your actions may not be immediate but will eventually lead you to better days!

TAKE ACTION NOW!

"If you can't fly then run, if you can't run then walk, if you can't walk then crawl, but whatever you do, you have to keep moving forward."

– Martin Luther King, Jr.

It has often been said that success begins "by just showing up." Many people miss the opportunity of a lifetime by registering for a seminar and then not attending it. For example, my wife and I once signed up for a real estate passive investing workshop located 30 miles from where we lived. I remember feeling sleepy and unmotivated to drive so far during a weekend morning. But off we went. We got so inspired at the workshop that we signed up for the full coaching program and made over $100,000 on our first two real estate deals. Imagine the missed opportunity if I had decided to sleep in that day!

No amount of intelligence, attitude, opportunities or wealth can ever produce anything without taking action. The same can be said for resilience. Below are some action items that will battle the temptation of laziness and help you overcome the very human inclination to procrastinate, which is often due to a tendency to seek comfort, attain perfection or avoid failure. Remember this: It's always better to start immediately and produce imperfect results than to never have tried at all.

ACTION ITEMS FOR ACHIEVING YOUR DREAMS

1. **Set an intention:** Any new venture grows from personal desires. Ask yourself deep questions, beginning with your "why," for pursuing habitual resilience. Your "why" must be deep, and from your heart and soul, for it will be the fuel that powers your engine to achieve your goals. Your thoughts become words; words become deeds; deeds become habits and habits become character. And character is everything.

    Be as specific as possible when writing your intentions so that you attain a clear vision of the action to be taken. Here is an example of a clear and specific intention:

    "Although my job doesn't allow me to express creativity, I will not dwell on this situation. Instead, I will start freelancing on Saturdays for 6 months and try out different careers to discover what I like and don't like to do, then reassess whether to stay in my job or start another profession on the side."

2. **Let your intentions marinate:** Once you have set a clear intention for yourself, take time each day to allow it to settle deeply into your mind. Reflect on these intentions and incorporate them into your thoughts by doing the following:

    a. Keep a journal: Write down ideas that had a positive impact on you or made you see things in a different light.

    b. Share your intentions: Talk to friends and family about your quest for resiliency and garner their support to help you commit and not quit.

    c. Create a written pledge: Unlike journaling, this is less of an investigation of feelings and more of a concrete promise to yourself. For example, say "I pledge to see every crisis as an opportunity to develop resilience." Place it where you will see it every day.

3. **Identify potential obstacles:** Think about any potential obstacles and write them down. Develop contingency plans to minimize the risk of outright failure. Most things never go according to plan! Once you realize this, you will be able to maintain a positive attitude, persevere and develop resilience. For example, if there is someone at work who constantly complains about their pay, can you change the topic of conversation to your company's superior culture?

4. **Determine what is achievable:** Let your dreams run wild. Dreams are the stuff great successes are made of. Balance big dreams with practical considerations. This allows you to avoid wasting precious time on frivolous or unrealistic dreams. Some important questions to ask yourself are:

a. "What is my plan? How am I going to get from A to B?"

b. "Will my family help me achieve this goal?"

c. "In which situations in my professional or family life can resilience be achieved?"

5. **Set a realistic timeline:** Change can be messy, unpredictable and non-linear. Expect three steps forward and one step back. Days quickly turn into weeks, months and years with little progress. Break down your goal of habitual resilience into mini-goals and create realistic deadlines. By doing this, you will be able to make steady progress.

6. **Stay focused on your dreams:** Develop the ability to zoom out from the weeds and stay focused on your dreams. Imagine being at the top of a mountain observing yourself in the valley preparing to walk up the mountain. Are you doing things that detract from your path? Are you looking for a nearby cave for a quick nap? Do you have the right equipment? Visualization can be helpful in staying focused on developing resilience when there are a lot of distractions in your life.

7. **Swap out old habits:** We're all guilty of picking up bad habits. Making lasting change in your life requires swapping out bad habits for good ones. Remember how it takes at least 30 days to develop a good habit or overcome a bad one. Remember the importance of starting small and of overcoming bad habits one step at a time.

8. **Stay the course:** The most important (and sometimes hardest thing to do) is to stick with it! We've all been there. You are creating change because you desire more positive outcomes. Whenever you want to give up, always come back to your "Why" and stay the course.

Resilience is one of the most beneficial character traits. It will benefit your body, mind, heart and soul for the rest of your life. Commit to handling challenging situations with courage and grace each day, and you will soon be on your way to living your best life and achieving your wildest dreams! By using the tools we have discussed, you will be on the path to resilience. So go ahead: Develop a positive attitude! Be an explorer! Go the extra mile! Never give up! And finally, take action NOW!

I hope this chapter has given you a good starting point on how to build resilience. I can't wait to further connect with you online or in person. It would be an honor to help a fellow hiker up the mountain of your dreams!

Connect with Tim today!

"The Salaried Investor Book: 7 Ways To Make More Money Without Quitting Your Job" Search "The Salaried Investor Book" on Facebook and join this exclusive group.

Find him on LinkedIn: @timdelosocpactp

Stay tuned for Tim's career coaching course and book of inspirational quotes… Coming soon!

You Are Not Your Scars™

ELLIE D. SHEFI

*"Step out of the history that is holding you back.
Step into the new story you are willing to create."*
– Oprah Winfrey

**Have you ever looked around and thought to yourself,
"How did I get here?"**

Do you feel powerless? Unseen? Unheard? Unvalued? Like you're living someone else's life? A life driven by someone else's dreams, desires, demands, labels, and expectations? A life dictated by your past? A life controlled by your circumstances?

I get it. I've lived that life. A life of stress, pain, emptiness, loneliness, and despair. A life of fatigue and weariness. A life where I so badly wanted to be seen, heard, valued, and loved—yet wasn't. A life where I desperately wanted things to be different, but felt hopelessly powerless to make them so. Then, slowly but surely, I began to learn the keys to freedom. Through almost five decades of getting back up every time life has knocked me down, I've developed tools to break free from external expectations, create an impervious mind, and live life on my terms. I'm here to help you do the same. With me ...

You are seen. You are heard. You are valued.

Who am I to guide you on your journey to an authentic, empowered life? I'm Ellie. I'm typically introduced as an attorney, entrepreneur, award-winning author, featured speaker, teacher, trainer, and coach, but I want to introduce myself to you as I truly am. I'm an abuse survivor, a rape survivor, and a former anorexic who still struggles with body dysmorphia. I've struggled financially, lived in my car, and eaten the food restaurants were throwing away at the end of the night. I'm a twice-divorced, childless, middle-aged woman. I'm a cancer survivor and a medical miracle. For over two decades, I've defied the doctors' death deadlines. I've had 13 major surgeries, and underneath my clothes, my body is covered in scars.

I have crawled, clawed, and scratched my way through fire after fire, and through it all, I have emerged a limitless thriver, problem solver, and opportunity creator, who chooses to live life with unending optimism. I have mastered turning fear into faith and pain into purpose. It's my life's mission to equip you with the resources you need to break free from the chains of your past and create the authentic and abundant life you design. Thank you for allowing me to be part of your journey.

While the lessons in this chapter are valuable to anyone seeking to make powerful and lasting changes to their lives, I'm especially speaking to the women of the world. Each of the stories and tools I share with you here is fortified with the wisdom and love of the extraordinary women who have helped me find my way. As you read this chapter and work through the exercises, you will be stepping into your power, and into a sisterhood of resilient and empowered women who are living life on their terms.

By allowing yourself to be fully present and vulnerable in these exercises, you will free yourself from the wounds and limiting stories of your past. I will show you how to shift your perspective, create empowering narratives, harness the power of gratitude, and be the designer of your destiny. From there, you will unearth what drives you, recalibrate your compass, and program your life's GPS so you can navigate to your ultimate destination—a life lived as your authentic and empowered self.

Your life is yours to create. The time is NOW.

YOU ARE NOT YOUR SCARS™

"I tell my story not because it is unique, but because it is not."
– Malala Yousafzai

Scars. We all have them. Some are visible. Others are not. Some we are conscious of. Others lurk in the shadows. Some are from childhood. Others have grown over the wounds adulthood and independence bring. Some are physical. Others are mental and emotional. Regardless of their type or origin, everyone has them. I have them. You have them. Your best friend has them. The person standing behind you in the line at the grocery store has them. The server who brings you your meal at a restaurant has them. The biggest stars in the world have them. We all have them.

Though our scars have shaped our histories and our life paths, they do not define us. Scars are stories of survival, of strength. Your scars are reminders that you are stronger than you ever thought possible—that you have persevered and overcome every obstacle that life has put before you. Your scars are reminders that you are a relentless force. You are unstoppable!

When you accept and even embrace your scars, you create space to define for yourself who you are, what you stand for, and what you want out of life. You can step into your power and create the life you desire. YOU GET TO CHOOSE! Choose to shed the past and never again allow external circumstances to define you. Choose to take control of your life—a life you design. Choose to live life on your own terms!

And, like scars, which are literally layer upon layer of healing strength, you, too, are the embodiment of resilience. You can intentionally and deliberately chart a new course for your life—a life that YOU define; that YOU create—a life where YOU decide your dreams, your desires, your passions, your values, and your vision for a life of impact, meaning, and purpose! So, welcome! You're here because you're ready. I'm here to empower you and give you the tools to succeed.

CHANGE YOUR STORY, CHANGE YOUR LIFE

> *"We delight in the beauty of the butterfly, but rarely admit the changes it has gone through to achieve that beauty."*
> – Maya Angelou

So, how do you live life by your design?

Words, and the meanings you assign them, are incredibly powerful. In fact, the words you attach to your experiences actually become your experiences!

Have you ever noticed that the more you tell people you're tired, the more tired you feel? The more you tell people you're stressed, the more stressed and overwhelmed you feel? The more you tell people a story about how someone betrayed you, the more betrayed and angry you feel? The words you use and the stories you create about a situation are more powerful than the situation itself! Your words, your thoughts, and your stories either empower you or imprison you. What stories are you telling yourself about things that have happened to you?

I know you can't choose what's happened to you. Believe me, I do. But what I also know is that when you change the story you tell yourself about what's happened to you, you change your life.

I'm not telling you to ignore the events of your life. They happened. No one can wave a magic wand and erase them from your life. What I am saying, though, is that when you change the words you use to describe your thoughts, feelings, and life events to reflect an empowering narrative, you take control and write your own story. You may be thinking, "That sounds great, but how does this work in real life?" Let me explain:

My friend is a blind woman who was born to a poor family in rural India. In her village, it was common for daughters to be sold into marriage for a dowry. Being born blind, her mother and father knew that she would not attract a high dowry and they could not afford to feed her. Without a proper dowry, feeding her meant that someone else would starve.

One day, her mother took her by the hand and led her to a bus stop and left her there. Abandoned. Frightened. Alone.

For years, this was my friend's reality. This was her life story, and she lived with all of the painful feelings that story brought up. She often told herself the story of how her parents were embarrassed by her, how she brought shame to her family, and how she was such a burden they had to cast her aside in order to be free from the shame and financial burden that this poor, disfigured, blind girl imposed upon them. She told herself the story that she was worth so little that she could easily be discarded. She told herself the story that she was unlovable and unworthy. All of these feelings created an overflowing well of anger, pain, and resentment within her.

This story defined her, until one day she made a powerful decision. She decided that this was not the story of her childhood. She decided to change her story and change her life. She shifted her perspective and took control of her narrative.

Today, if you ask her what her life story is, she will tell you that she was born to a loving mother and father in a poor village in rural India. She will tell you that, being blind, her parents knew that even if they were able to find a husband who would be willing to pay a dowry for her, she might not be treated well. They worried for her future. The only way they could help her have a better life was to let her go.

So one day her mother summoned all of the courage within her so that she could do what she felt was the right thing for her beloved child. She took her daughter by the hand and led her to a well-lit bus stop near the police station, where she was sure to be found by a kind policeman. Not wanting to frighten her child or draw attention to what was happening right away, she sat her beloved daughter on the bench and quietly walked away. With tears in her eyes, she didn't look back.

As her mother had hoped, a kind policeman found her and took her to the safety of an orphanage, where she was adopted by an incredible family in Canada. She has been more loved by her adopted family than she ever thought possible. She is thriving every single day—all because her loving mother selflessly released her to a better life. Her mother loved her enough to let her go, and for that she is eternally grateful.

My friend's story is a powerful example. Although the events of her life are what they are—her mother left her as a very young blind girl at a bus stop near a police station in rural India—her story reminds us of the power of the words we use and the meanings we give them. As my friend so poignantly demonstrates, you can use the story you tell yourself about events in your life to either keep yourself in an emotional prison, or you can take the key and set yourself free. Changing the meaning she attached to the events of her past set her free. For the first time in her life, she allowed herself to feel loved, worthy, enough, wanted, and valued. Reframing her story allowed her to replace anger and resentment with empathy, compassion, and gratitude. Her shift in meaning didn't change the facts of what happened, but by changing her story, she found a new life, and a new future.

When you change your perspective, everything shifts. It's like knocking down the first domino. One falls, and then the next and then the next and then the next, until you have knocked down the chain of pain, the chain of anger, the chain of resentment, and the chain of unworthiness. Once these chains have been broken and you've chosen to replace them with gratitude, joy, forgiveness, compassion, and love, you're empowered to take control and tell your true story—the story you write!

YOU ARE YOUR SOURCE

"You are the designer of your destiny; you are the author of your story."
– Lisa Nichols

Does it feel like someone else is writing your life story? Telling you what to do and who to be?

Smile.

Be a doting yet wise mother, a caring daughter, a supportive sister, and a loving wife ... without exception or excuse ... 24/7.

Be successful in your career, but simultaneously be a domestic goddess.

Smile.

Be independent, handle everything, remain poised, and keep it together.

Be skinny, beautiful, and perfectly put together, but don't be high-maintenance.

Smile.

Be an active member of the PTA, your place of worship, and your community.

Be confident, but not bossy.

Smile.

Be completely accessible and supportive whenever your family and friends need you.

Be fun, funny, and liked by all, but don't overshadow anyone.

SMILE!!!

Sound familiar? Now, imagine breaking free from the chains of labels, expectations, and external demands. What will your story look like once you begin to write it? No matter what your life story so far has been, you have the power to turn the page, grab your favorite pen, and write a new story. You are the master of your life. You can define for yourself who you want to be, what you want to stand for, and what you want your life to be. YOU GET TO CHOOSE.

Claim what you want today, right now, and go for it! Create space for all of the magnificence that is you by shedding the expectations, demands, and labels that others have imposed upon you. Shed all of the beliefs about yourself that others have placed on you. The greatness that is you shines when you stop letting others tell you how that greatness should look, feel, and behave. You don't need anyone else to create the life you want—you have it all within you. YOU ARE YOUR SOURCE. There is nothing holding you back from starting right this minute. I believe in you.

I've done it, and I know you can too. I've picked myself up in moments when I didn't think I could, and I've decided time and time again to change my story, shift my perspective, and take control of my life. Since the moment I made that first powerful decision, with each subsequent twist and turn, I've consciously chosen empowering meanings and perspectives, and I've intentionally placed myself in the driver's seat, grabbed hold of that steering wheel, and hit the gas pedal toward destinations I set.

But it hasn't always been that way.

What was my turning point, you ask? I'm a domestic violence survivor. Things got bad. So bad that my health deteriorated and my life literally depended on the help of others to get me out. My removal from the situation took four police officers and my dad driving the getaway car. Two officers pulled me out of my apartment, two officers held my ex-husband back, and my dad stepped hard on the gas the second the officers put me in his car.

I was put into hiding and, for a while, I became a ghost. I was placed in a home with a man I didn't know. I was terrified. I barely left my room and had lost all ability to make a decision. Every single day for the rest of the year, I ate the exact same thing for breakfast, lunch, and dinner because no one told me what to eat and I simply was not capable of making my own decisions or functioning independently.

Then, one day, after months of intense trauma therapy, something shifted in me. I finally understood that, if things were going to get better, I had to make a choice. I had to be the one to decide that my life was worth more, that I was worth more. I began changing my story. Instead of seeing myself as the girl whose future had been snatched from her, I decided to see my situation as an opportunity.

"I am complete ashes," I told myself. "This is ground zero for my life. What an incredible opportunity I have to start over from scratch and rebuild myself into exactly who I want to be. What an amazing gift that, in starting over, I get to define for myself who I will be, what I will stand for, and how I will live my life from this point forward. What freedom!"

I recognized right then and there that my experiences were a blessing. I finally understood that I was powerful beyond measure and that I actually had control over my life in all aspects—even those that I had thus far felt powerless to control. I realized that I had the power to write my own story, the way I wanted it to be … not my parents, not my past, not society, and not labels placed on me by an outside observer. Me. I had the power! I became my own source.

A lot has happened in the decades since my rescue and resurrection. I've continued to write my own narrative through every obstacle life has thrown my way. You see, just because you decide to take control of your narrative, your perspective, and your life once, doesn't mean that you're magically in this impervious, unshakable state of perpetual power and positivity. Writing your story is a daily decision; a daily practice.

Every moment of every day, you have the opportunity to write your story. Every moment of every day, you have the opportunity to reclaim your power, recalibrate your compass, and put yourself in the driver's seat of your life.

Sometimes finding the empowering meaning and perspective in events and circumstances takes more work than others, but it's always worth it.

Take control of your narrative. By choosing to do this every single day, external circumstances no longer define you. The views of others no longer define you. YOU DEFINE YOU.

Remember, you are your own source of strength, light, inspiration, and power. Choose an empowering perspective and write the story you want to tell. You are the author of your life.

THE POWER OF GRATITUDE, PERSPECTIVE, AND MEANING

> *"The more you praise and celebrate your life,*
> *the more there is in life to celebrate."*
> – Oprah Winfrey

Being able to control perspective and meaning is the key to your ability to constantly create the life of your choosing. As you've seen with the examples I've shared, your words control your meanings, your meanings control your thoughts and stories, your thoughts and stories control your emotions, your emotions control your actions, and your actions control your results. When you can change your story, you can change your life; and when you can shift your perspective, you can claim your power.

Now, let's talk about the power of gratitude. Yes, gratitude. Have you ever noticed that when you allow yourself to feel truly grateful about something, you cannot simultaneously feel angry, anxious, fearful, worried, or frustrated?

Go ahead—try it. Think of something for which you are truly and deeply grateful. Put yourself back in that beautiful moment. Notice how you feel. Notice the warmth. Notice the sense of peace. Notice the love. Notice the joy. Notice the appreciation. Of course, you can feel anger, worry, fear, or frustration before and after you feel grateful, but it's impossible to feel negative emotions and gratitude at the same time.

Gratitude is an incredibly powerful force. On the days when you feel like the walls are caving in, use gratitude as the hook to pull you to safety. In the moments when you are weary and feel like you just can't go on, find something in your life to be grateful for. Something ... anything. It's there! Give thanks for the breath you take, the roof over your head, the bed that you sleep in, the blanket that keeps you warm. Give thanks for the senses you have, for the electricity you have, for the running water you have, for the food you eat. Seek your blessings, and feel grateful. Feeling grateful interrupts whatever negative emotion you're experiencing long enough to help you shift your perspective and fuel your strength to persevere.

I've spent the better part of two decades living in and out of hospitals, fighting for my life. At one point, I grew tired of the pain, tired of the struggle, and tired of the constant fight to survive. I was giving up. I had had enough. I was done fighting the doctors' death deadlines. Then one day, everything changed. It was a day I had to have another excruciating test. When it was time for me to go for testing, the porter came to get me from my room and wheeled my wheelchair down hallways that he had never taken me through before.

He wheeled me through the hallways of the area in the hospital where everyone was either paralyzed from the neck down and on a ventilator, or in a coma and on a ventilator. I looked into room after room and realized that any one of those patients would give anything to feel the pain I was feeling. In an instant, I realized my pain was an incredible blessing, and I was so lucky to be able to feel it travel around my body. In that moment, I made a choice to once again take control of my life. I thanked God that I still had nerves that were connected and synapses that were firing as they should. What a gift! I turned my pity-party into gratitude and my weariness became resolve. I became flooded with gratitude for my body and all it provided me.

The ability to find and feel true gratitude in the midst of chaos, pain, despair, and darkness is the ultimate mind hack. It is a powerful tool—one that can be learned. Just as you can train your mind to assign empowering meanings to life's events and you can train your mind to frame things with a positive, powerful perspective, you can also train your mind to operate from a place of gratitude. Changing your meaning takes practice. Changing your perspective takes practice. And living in gratitude takes practice. The more work you do in your gratitude practice, the stronger it will be. It's like any other skill you've honed in your life. You can do it!

I am truly grateful for all of the challenges I have faced in this life because they have made me who I am today. I am a powerhouse and a force to be reckoned with, and I am grateful for all that I have allowed myself to become. Who are you choosing to become? I am grateful that you have allowed me to be part of your journey, and I am excited to celebrate your strength, your progress, and your journey to a full and authentic you!

YOUR LIFE INVENTORY

> *"Don't let anyone define you. You define yourself."*
> – Billie Jean King

Let's begin by assessing where you are in your life right now. Take inventory of your life in a deep and meaningful way so that you're clear about where you're starting. Be honest with yourself about the story of your life as it currently is.

Consider: How would you describe yourself to others? How would others describe you? When you talk about your life, what do you say? How do you describe your life? What life events have shaped you? What effect has each had? What's been your biggest obstacle? What's currently holding you back? If you had to sum up your life in one word, what word would that be?

Knowing your starting point is the first step in recalibrating your compass and programming the GPS for your new life. After all, when you want to go somewhere, what does your GPS need to know? Just two simple pieces of information: your starting point and your destination! Soon, you'll begin defining your destination, but for now, focus on taking a raw, honest inventory of your life in its current form.

YOUR WHY

> *"There is a powerful driving force inside every human being that, once unleashed, can make any vision, dream, or desire a reality."*
> – Tony Robbins

Now that you've completed the first step in taking your life inventory and you know where you're starting from, let's dive into the catalyst for change—your why. As powerful as meaning, perspective, and gratitude are in your life's journey, the ultimate driving force you have is your why. Your why is both your fuel and your anchor—it propels you forward and it keeps you centered. Understanding and connecting to your core why gives you an inexhaustible, replenishable, on-demand source of strength, resolve, drive, and focus.

Your core why is the absolute, most fundamental knowledge you need to create life on your own terms. How many people can you think of who live life on auto-pilot, aimlessly floating down the river of life, experiencing each day as it happens? Knowing your core why provides guidance in times of uncertainty. It allows you to consciously align your beliefs and actions with every choice you make. Your choices become intentional. When your why is at the root of your dreams, desires, goals, choices, and actions, you take control and live your life with purpose, on purpose.

Pause and reflect: What drives you? What is your core why? Do you know? If you haven't yet done so, take time for introspection. Dig deep and search for your core why. Ask yourself: "What's most important to me in life?" Really think about it. Now, whatever your answer is, dig deeper—ask yourself why that is the most important thing to you in life. Keep digging! You're two layers in! Keep repeating the process, each time asking why that answer is the most important thing in life to you. Continue digging deeper and deeper with each answer, until you hit your core why. There's no particular number of layers you need to strip away to get to your core why; just keep digging until you get there. You'll know it when you hit it. It's undeniable. It's powerful. It's emotional.

My friend recently completed this exercise. I'll share her process with you as an example of how this works in a practical sense:

Q: *What's the most important thing to you in life?*
A: *I want to be successful.*

Q: *Why is being successful the most important thing to you in life?*
A: *Because I want to own a big house.*

Q: Why is owning a big house the most important thing to you in life?

A: Because I want my parents to be able to live with me.

Q: Why is having your parents live with you the most important thing to you in life?

A: Because I never want my parents to stress over money again, like they did when I was growing up.

Q: Why is having your parents never stress over money again the most important thing to you in life?

A: Because I want to show them how much I love them, how much I appreciate them, and how grateful I am for everything they sacrificed for me. I want to provide for them and take care of them like they did for me.

You see, at the beginning of the exercise, my friend thought her why, her fuel, her purpose for the choices she was making and the actions she was taking, was to be successful and have a big house. But when she dug deep, she realized that her real reason and purpose, her core why, her true fuel for everything she did, was to give back to her parents—to show them love, appreciation, and gratitude; and to provide for them and take care of them. Notice the power of her core why!

Your core why will get you out of bed on the days you think you can't. It will give you the strength to persevere when you are weary. It will give you the drive to push through all obstacles. When you are driven by a clear core why, never again will you allow yourself to be defined by someone else's labels, dreams, desires, or expectations. Never again will you allow your past to dictate your present or control your future. Never again will you be your scars.

When you are driven by a clear core why, your scars become your strength. Your scars become your proof to yourself and to the world that you are more powerful than all of the things that have ever happened to you. Your why gives you the strength to rise, and rise again, to get up and keep going when it seems impossible to do so. Your why makes you resilient. Your why makes you relentless. Your why drives you to reach the heights of your limitless potential, and to live the life you desire.

With your why at your very core, you are equipped to navigate the next leg of your journey with clarity, strength, focus, and determination.

YOUR JOURNEY TO AN AUTHENTIC, EMPOWERED YOU

> *"Your time is limited, so don't waste it living someone else's life."*
> – Steve Jobs

You've taken your life inventory and know where you're starting. You understand your why, or are doing the work to understand it. What's next?

Create an authentic, empowered you in three steps:
1. Claim what your life will be.
2. Claim who you choose to be.
3. Claim your legacy. Let's get to it!

Write Your Eulogy

Imagine you've come to the end of a life lived on your own terms—a life you've defined, a life you've designed, a life you've created, and a life you've chosen. What would people say about you and the life you lived? Write your eulogy.

"Wait, what?!? You want me to do what?!"

Yes, I am asking you to write your own eulogy. Why would I do that? Because writing your eulogy empowers you with unmatched clarity and purpose to live the life you want to live. Writing your eulogy is like programming your life's ultimate GPS. Write your own life story, exactly the way you want it to be told. What does living your best life look like? Feel like? What did you accomplish? What did you contribute? Dig deep and don't hold back. You are the author. Write the life story of your dreams. Go for it!

When you're writing your eulogy, answer this question:

WHY DID YOUR LIFE MATTER?

It's a tough question, I know. If you get stuck, start by writing the eulogy that would be written about you right now, if you died today. Be honest. Now read it. Is that the story you want told? What parts would you change? How would you change them?

Armed with that clarity, write a new eulogy to be read at the end of the life you design, claim, and live from this point forward; a life at the end of which friends, family, and strangers can't help but proclaim: "Wow, now that was a life well-lived!"

Claim that amazing life you've written about in your eulogy. Feel it. Experience it. Believe that you are achieving all that you desire, and witness the changes within yourself. You're walking differently. You're dressing in a way that is unapologetically you. You're making different decisions. You're standing guard at the gate of your mind, using empowering words and assigning empowering meanings. You don't shy away from the difficult stuff, because nothing is more important than being you and living the life you've chosen. That life becomes this life; it is the destination you programmed into your life's GPS.

Now you know where you're starting and you know where you're heading. You're fueled by your why, and you're equipped with the powerful tools of meaning, perspective, and gratitude. You're on your way to living the authentic, empowered life that you've designed—a life truly well-lived. The journey has begun!

Develop Your Soul Signature

Next, it's time to develop your Soul Signature. "Develop my Soul Signature?" Indeed! Your Soul Signature is the unique imprint that only you can leave on this world. It is your chosen essence—who you define yourself to be at your very core. Take some time to really think about who you want to be from this point forward. Who do you need to become in order to live the life you've envisioned? Who is the person eulogized? Describe her in vivid detail.

Think of your Soul Signature as your personal mission statement or your personal brand statement. It is the representation of the values and beliefs you embrace. It is the heart of your magnificence. It is the spirit of YOU. What do you want it to say? How do you want to be seen? As you step into your power and clearly define your chosen identity, how do you want to be known? Write your Soul Signature.

Once you've written your Soul Signature, post it where you will see it daily! Post it on the bathroom mirror, on the refrigerator door, and on the visor in your car. Read it often. Let it be a tangible reminder of who you choose to be. Never again will you be who someone else dictates. You define for yourself who you are, and what you stand for. You are your Soul Signature!

Create Your Legacy

When you were writing your eulogy, I asked you to envision life as you ultimately claim it to be and to think about why, at the end of it all, your life mattered. Now, I ask you to take that one step further and think about the legacy you want to leave behind. When designing your life and your legacy, claim your power and your purpose. What is the purpose of your life? How will you fulfill that purpose in such a way that you leave an imprint for generations to come? What impact do you want to make on this world and the people in it? The mark you make on this world is yours to choose—choose powerfully!

WHAT IS YOUR LEGACY?

Write it out! Be as specific and detailed as you can possibly be.

Now that you know what your legacy will be, it's time to break it down so that you can create a roadmap for making it happen! Write down the components of your legacy (family? faith? friends? contribution or service? work?). Next, evaluate where you are in life with each component. Be honest with yourself. When you're clear on your starting point for each one, you can create attainable benchmarks so that you can continually progress toward building YOUR legacy.

As you continue creating an authentic, empowered you, and writing your chosen life story, always remember: Your life is yours. Your legacy is yours. Your chosen future awaits. Step into your power and claim life on your own terms NOW.

LIFE HAPPENS FOR YOU, NOT TO YOU

> *"Freeing yourself was one thing, claiming ownership of that freed self was another."*
> – Toni Morrison

Everything I've talked about leads to this—the ultimate key to creating the authentic, empowered life you define for yourself. You now know the power of your words and the meanings you ascribe to them. You now know the power of shifting your perspective and controlling the narrative you tell yourself. You now know that when you change your story, you change your life. Now, you are equipped to know, with absolute certainty, that life happens for you, not to you.

"Wait, what? Say that again!?"

LIFE HAPPENS FOR YOU, NOT TO YOU!

What exactly does that mean? It is a belief that—when held with absolute, unwavering certainty—allows you to train yourself to find the good in things, to find the lesson in things, to find the blessing in things. It's easy to find the negative in situations or events. It's not always so easy to find the good. The key is to train yourself to find the good, because what you focus on, you feel, and because what you focus on, you'll find. (Try it ... look around and notice everything that's brown. What did you see? Now look around again, and notice everything that's red. What did you see? Why didn't you notice all the red stuff when you were looking for brown stuff? Simple—you find what you focus on!)

As Tony Robbins says, "What's wrong is always available, but so is what's right." Embracing a "life happens for me, not to me" mentality necessitates that you train your brain to seek and create positive situations and opportunities that serve you. When you train yourself to focus on the good, you find the good. When you train yourself to focus on your blessings, you see how blessed you are. When you train yourself to focus on solutions and opportunities, you find solutions and opportunities, and you're able to continue building the life and legacy you've designed.

When, no matter what, you can look at all that happens in your life and know with every fiber of your being that everything is happening for you, not to you, you have truly taken control over your life experience. You are no longer your scars. You have set yourself free.

Free, empowered, and equipped, you are unstoppable. You are unbreakable. You are resilient. And you are limitless.

THE JOURNEY CONTINUES

"For me, becoming isn't about arriving somewhere or achieving a certain aim. I see it instead as forward motion, a means of evolving, a way to reach continuously toward a better self. The journey doesn't end."
– Michelle Obama

You did it! You stepped into your power. You have clarity and focus about what the life you claim for yourself looks like, and you know why your life matters. You've grabbed a fresh notebook, taken hold of your favorite pen, and begun writing your new life story—one that is authentically and unapologetically yours. As a member of a community of women who are also authoring their life stories, you are not alone. You are a part of a sisterhood that spans the globe.

Welcome to You Are Not Your Scars™, a global movement that empowers and supports women who are ready to let go of their old lives, turn the page, and write their new life stories. I'm grateful that you're here! I look forward to supporting you on your journey and celebrating your milestones along the way. I honor you, and the resiliency you've shown in surviving all the obstacles you've already faced in life. I celebrate the voice inside you that knows you're worthy of so much more—the voice that believes that you can, and will, live life on your own terms.

I am so proud to be here with you on this journey. Together, we are limitless. Together, we thrive! As a community of creators who choose to never again be defined by our scars—by external experiences, expectations, and circumstances—we're claiming our narratives, taking control of our lives, and emerging as the relentless thrivers we choose to be. *You are not alone. You are part of the collective we.*

One of the best gifts you can give yourself is the gift of a safe, supportive, and intentional community to journey alongside you and celebrate you as you step into your power and create your new life! To help you do so, I have created a FREE Facebook community where you can connect with other women who are determined to define for themselves who they are, what they stand for, and what their lives will be.

Join our FREE Facebook community today: @YouAreNotYourScars

Your sisterhood and I stand ready to welcome you and support you with compassion, resources, and actionable tools you can use to create the future you desire and live life on your terms. Join us! Let's walk forward together. Your sisterhood and I await!

To learn more about You Are Not Your Scars™ or connect with me directly, head to: www.EllieShefi.com

There, you'll find valuable resources, and information about all of the ways I can serve you powerfully, including courses, workshops, and coaching. I look forward to continuing our journey together!

Unlocking the Secret to Success

Discovering the Power of Emotional Intelligence

RAV BAINS

WHAT IS EMOTIONAL INTELLIGENCE?

What is an emotion?

An emotion is a feeling we get as a result of something that has triggered us. This trigger can be internal or external; in other words, something that we think, see, hear, speak or do. For example, you might see two people arguing, and that could arouse some emotion in you. An example of an internal trigger could be that you think of something in the past that was negative, and this has brought up an emotion in you. The other important factor to remember is that an emotion can be strong or weak. The strength of the emotion will depend on your interpretation of what you've thought, seen, heard, spoke or done. Since we all have different values and belief systems, the event, whether internal or external, is "neutral." Why is this important to understand? Because you have a choice as to how to react to the thing that has happened! Now you might ask how this is possible. If I see a car accident how can that be neutral? Isn't it bound to evoke an emotion? Well, what is the likelihood that ten people who witnessed the accident will have the same reaction? They won't. Their reactions could range from very strong to slight, to no reaction at all. So, it's not the event, but rather your interpretation of that event that will determine the emotion. One of the reasons you blame the event for your emotional reaction is that it all happens in a fraction of a second! As a result, you confuse the trigger (the event) with your emotional reaction, which is actually determined by you. This topic always becomes an interesting conversational point in my seminars, which is great because it allows for rich understanding of emotions and triggers. The important thing to remember is that life has no meaning until we give it meaning.

What triggers an emotion?

Now that we have touched on emotions and triggers, the next critical question for you to ask is what triggers your emotions. Understanding this question is fundamental to understanding your personal and professional success or failure. You see, people never stop to think why they have an emotional reaction to something. In fact, did you know that 90% of the population don't think? (Earl Nightingale) Just because they have thoughts (which are often haphazard), they believe they are thinking. Thinking is the deliberate, conscious awareness of the thoughts you are having, and deciding what thoughts you actually want to have. The other fundamental mistake people make is that they think they are their thoughts. We aren't our thoughts. We are aware of our thoughts, so we can't be the thoughts. Now at this point you might feel a little confused.

That's ok, it will become clearer as you read on. It's critical that you get to know what triggers you. It could be what people say or do, or certain circumstances, situations or events. It's also important to be aware of the type of emotion or feeling you're getting in those situations and circumstances. These emotions will determine how you act and react. Are they positive or negative? Are they pleasurable or painful? These questions will help to determine whether you're making good judgments or not. They will also determine whether you're responding or reacting to the person, situation or circumstances. One of the other fundamental factors to remember is that human beings can trigger an emotional reaction simply by thinking bad thoughts—without anyone else interfering. So, you can get into a bad mood all by yourself!

Emotions drive behavior

Many people seem to think that their circumstances cause them to react to things, and that's why they have an emotional reaction. As a result, they constantly blame what's happening around them, which is external to them. In my coaching sessions I've heard so many individuals complain about their partner, the kids, the boss or their team at work. It's as if they think that changing what's around them will allow them to be happy or in a better mood. This means no more emotional reaction. Well, if you've been following the earlier reading, then you'll have remembered that all events are neutral, and only you are in control of your feelings and emotions. Therefore, the mood you're in or the emotional reaction you're having to a situation or event will determine how you behave! For example, if you're in a bad mood, what's the likelihood you're going to be at your best at home or in the workplace? We can safely assume you're not going to be! What many people fail to realize is that emotions, not circumstances, drive behavior. So, how you're feeling or what kind of emotional state you're in will determine your performance and your leadership. This means that if you want to change your own or someone else's behavior you must get to the root cause of the emotion that's driving them or you, otherwise you'll be focusing your energies on the symptoms instead of causes and, as a result, be less effective in your efforts. This is one of the key elements to understand as part of EI.

Definition of EI

Now that we've established what emotions are, what triggers emotions and that emotions drive behavior, we can conclude that *EI is one's ability to understand one's emotions—what triggers them, what circumstances cause the trigger and how to regulate the emotions.* By doing this there is a good chance that you'll make better, more thoughtful decisions and have a positive impact on those around you. This means better performance by you, and the role modeling of good personal leadership.

WHAT IS WISDOM?

Wisdom is having the knowledge of what is right or true, coupled with just judgment regarding an action to be taken. The most famous example of this is the story of two women who came to King Solomon, each claiming to be the mother of a certain infant. Knowing that only one could be the true mother, King Solomon decreed that the baby be cut in half and one part given to each woman. The true mother, unwilling to have her baby hurt in any way, revoked her claim. Solomon knew this would happen and, thus, awarded the child to that woman.

Intelligence versus Wisdom

King Solomon had to understand intelligence in order to make the decision he did … He had to be prepared to go through with his decree. And he also had to know how the true mother would react. So, on the surface, it would seem that both intelligence and emotional intelligence are necessary for wisdom. However, if we accept that the two women were intelligent in their own way, it quickly becomes apparent that intelligence is not necessary for wisdom.

Why is this important?

Thinking is the deliberate, conscious awareness of the thoughts you're having and then deciding what thoughts you want to have. This is the exact opposite of what most people do. Most people base their actions on how they feel in the moment. They don't take time to rationalize the situation and choose an appropriate thought.

WHY DO ORGANIZATIONS NEED EMOTIONAL INTELLIGENCE?

Because there are:

- **Challenges in individual behavior** … Once Emotional Intelligence is understood by individuals in organizations, their behavior changes dramatically. They stop reacting and start to respond thoughtfully to situations.

- **Challenges in building relationships** ... If employees are unable to cooperate with each other, this will affect organizational performance. Once people start to grasp the concept and competences of self-awareness, cooperation and harmony, it will lead to better results.

- **Challenges in teamwork** ... Teamwork is critical for success; however, too often individuals in teams fall into the "right wrong trap!" and individuals quickly start to take positions. Once people understand that it's all emotional, they start to focus on outcomes and results.

- **Challenges in managing change** ... Organizations struggle in implementing change, and employees often resist. Fear is a big factor in change management, as people focus on what they will lose as opposed to what they will gain. People start to 'awfulize,' but once they understand that it's the relationship between the emotional mind and the thinking mind that is driving the fear, resistance disappears.

- **Challenges in achieving organizational goals** ... Employees often struggle with their values versus the organization's values. They often forget what their Personal Leadership Responsibility is in the organization. Understanding the philosophy of Emotional Intelligence and personal accountability puts them back on the right track.

- **Challenges in understanding 'soft skills!'** ... Organizations spend millions of dollars on driving hard for goals and results, but remain weak on developing the soft skills required by individuals and teams. They fail to realize that it's the 'soft stuff' that makes the 'hard stuff' easier! Once individuals and teams grasp this concept, they excel in all areas of their lives and get engaged actively in achieving organizational results.

The main thing to remember about Emotional Intelligence is that it can be taught, improved and used within your company to create a healthy workplace, motivate employees and achieve your goals. It's definitely a strong tool that can put you out in front of your competition. So, get from being a good organization to a great organization!

UNDERSTANDING EMOTIONS AS VIBRATIONS

One of the failures of our learning is that no one has explained to us that emotions are actual vibrations in the body. When we are angry, we don't say "I have a negative vibration" we say "I am angry!" In other words, we have made the emotion part of who we are and, as a result, we do not pay attention to the vibration. We don't realize that it's a vibration, and that we aren't our vibrations. We are aware of our vibrations. I know this might be a little confusing, BUT this is one of the keys to really grasping what is happening to us emotionally. As a result, we'll have a chance to manage our emotions and hence our behavior.

It's critical to be in tune with what is happening in the body, and paying attention when there is a change in this vibration, because then you'll know you're having a reaction to something. I can't stress enough the importance of this fact. Start paying attention to the sensations/vibrations in your body. Stop living from the neck upwards, just in the mind!

I believe you aren't going to get this important piece of information from any other emotional intelligence book or trainer.

THINK ABOUT WHAT YOU'RE THINKING

We very rarely pay any attention to our thoughts. The average person doesn't understand the importance of thinking. People assume this is an activity that just happens and that they really don't have any control over it. Wrong! If you want to change your life, then start paying attention to what you're constantly thinking about. Are your thoughts negative or positive? Why is this important? Well, thoughts arouse emotions. Earl Nightingale, in 1960, said that "90% of people simply don't think!" You see, you need to understand that activity in the mind isn't thinking. We're constantly thinking about shopping lists, work, picking the kids up, cooking, and on and on we go! Not that this isn't important, but you need to understand that you're not your thoughts. You are, however, aware of your thoughts and therefore can choose what you think about. Negative thoughts will trigger negative emotions. Conversely, positive thoughts will trigger positive emotions, which in turn puts us in a better state of mind. We as humans have so habituated negative thinking that we have normalized it. So we pay no attention to what we're thinking and how it is affecting our behavior and performance. Understanding the importance of your thoughts, which give rise to emotions, is critical in changing your behavior. Managing your thinking and your emotions will lead to better management of your behavior. Remember, thoughts arouse emotions.

What is thinking?

Thinking is conscious and it's active. Think of it as internal speech (requires language). Sometimes that inner conversation appears to come unbidden or automatically; this would be subconscious thought. But it is during conscious and active thought that thinking takes on a whole new role. Here we can focus our thoughts to solve a problem. We can plan, design and, quite literally, create. This is where we can purposefully produce our thoughts and put some form to them. In simpler words, thinking is the action of using one's mind to produce thoughts.

90% of the people don't think

It's true; most people don't think. They go through their days on automatic, their thoughts being a reaction to what's happening around them and to them, rather than being a purposeful response. No wonder, though. The Socratic method is no longer taught in schools, and the young people of today don't seem to understand the importance of the "question." If you ask yourself (your mind) a question, the mind will always answer. Ask a great question, and you'll always get a great response. In fact, it's the act of questioning that creates our thoughts. So, think what will happen to a person who doesn't understand the importance of questions. Something happens, and random, or at least reactive, thoughts appear. Negative questions abound. *Why is this happening to me? What's going on? Who does he think he is? Where does this leave me?* Get the picture? What if this person had responded rather than reacted? The questions asked might appear like this: *This is interesting: how can what's happening serve me? Do I understand the situation properly, or will he clarify it for me? He certainly has some strong opinions: I wonder what his experience is in this area and if he would be interested in sharing his story and his reasoning? I think I'll ask him. Can't hurt, right?*

Why is this important?

The questions we ask will determine what we say and do. They are like the programs we feed our computer so that it can manipulate the raw data it receives in a way that is useful to us. You're the operator or programmer of your mind. You don't want to fall asleep on the job, do you? Then learn to ask yourself questions designed to get your mind used to generating specific words and actions so that they become a habit you can call on in many different situations. I call them rituals.

Thoughts arouse emotions

One of the most wonderful aspects of thought is that it can arouse emotions. You can discover which words or thoughts elicit emotions that can work for you in a difficult situation, then you can practice calling up those emotions. I'm talking about positive emotions like excitement, joy, happiness, and peace.

COMPETENCES OF EMOTIONAL INTELLIGENCE

There are many different views and opinions on the competences of Emotional Intelligence. I've found the following to be the best examples to describe the important competences.

Self-awareness is the foundation on which all other competences build on. Often, we don't take the time to disengage from day-to-day activity to review what has happened to us.

Example ... Before you go to bed at night, take the time to review your day. Ask questions like: *What were the positives? Which of my goals were achieved? What happened to make the day memorable?* Once you feel your review is complete, set your mind to work, planning tomorrow's day. You should write your goals down.

Example ... How can you really understand your stress levels if you don't spend some quiet time posing and answering questions designed to put your focus on the stress you feel in each large muscle mass? So, think back to a time when you felt totally relaxed and the stress literally bled from your body. What did that feel like? Compare that feeling to the one in the muscle mass we've been talking about. Clench those muscles for a count of ten and release. Does the feeling in the muscles match what you remembered? Not quite? Clench the muscles for another 10 seconds and release. Immediately notice how the muscles feel. Now do this with all the large muscles in your body, beginning with your head and working downward to your feet.

Make sure you're doing your best to match the feeling of relaxation you remembered. Breathe in when you clench, breathe out when you release. You can even pretend you're releasing the air through the muscle you just released. Do you feel yourself settling into your chair or your bed? Keep practicing and one day soon you'll find yourself completely relaxed.

Self-assessment is the ability to honestly assess one's strengths and weakness. This has to be done skillfully. It's an opportunity to review what you're naturally good at and what the opportunities are for self-improvement. Self-assessment does not mean beating yourself up! But, rather, it's thoughtful self-reflection that adds value in increasing your awareness about yourself and how you interact with your environment.

Again, use questions to elicit the thoughts you're after. *What did I do well today? What skills and talents did I use? What could I have done better? How?*

Managing Emotion

I've heard emotion referred to as a wild stallion that must be tamed. Thoughts generate emotions; emotions generate thoughts. Of the two possibilities, which seems more useful to you? Thoughts generating emotions, right? You have the reins: it's up to you to teach the stallion what that means, that you're in control.

It's much easier to choose useful thoughts that generate positive, supporting emotions than it is to control the thoughts evoked by powerful, negative emotions. Think about it … you always have a choice. You can ask questions that create thoughts that will evoke useful emotions or you can be overrun by thoughts that boil up unbidden from out of control negative emotion. You can tame the wild stallion or it can cast you into the dirt.

How is this emotion working for me? What thoughts can I choose that will evoke a better emotional response? What's good about this situation, and how can it serve me? Such questions are designed to focus on positive thoughts, emotions and results rather than reacting blindly to whatever emotion is elicited by the situation at hand.

Emotional Intelligence can be taught, improved and used within your company to achieve your goals. It is definitely a strong tool that can put you out in front of your competition. For more information or to book a seminar for your company, contact me at **ravsbains1@gmail.com**.

FINAL NOTE

The most important thing you can take away from this chapter is: **Life has no meaning other than what we give it**. A woman at a party stumbles and falls. One person is concerned that the woman might have been hurt by the fall. A second person starts laughing (because he noticed that the contents of the woman's drink flew into the face of someone he doesn't like very much).

In this situation, a woman fell. This has no meaning without context, hence the reactions of the two witnesses. They both put the fall into a specific context and then assigned meaning. The first witness saw the fall in the context of the woman becoming injured. This triggered the emotion of concern. The second witness saw the fall in the context of someone he disliked getting a drink in the face. This triggered the emotion of delight.

The trick, the wisdom we must develop, is understanding that we have FREE WILL to choose whatever it is we want to think, feel, say or do. It doesn't matter what has happened, because it means nothing until, and if, we make it so.

Remember ... "People will often forget what you said, but they will never forget how you made them feel." - Maya Angelou

To book a seminar for your organization, contact
Rav Bains at **ravsbains1@gmail.com**

www.ingramcontent.com/pod-product-compliance
Lightning Source LLC
Chambersburg PA
CBHW061304110426
42742CB00012BA/2048